Terrorism and
Global Security

About the Book and Author

In the seven years since this book was first published, the threat of nuclear terrorism has increased dramatically. The enormously destructive potential of nuclear technology inevitably raises the specter of the use of nuclear explosives or radioactivity by insurgent groups. In this completely revised and updated edition, Professor Beres explores the political bases of terrorism by considering the factors that might foster nuclear terrorism, the forms it could take, and the probable consequences of such acts. New to this edition is the author's examination of the essential distinctions between lawful insurgencies and terrorism, as well as his analysis of the impact of recent U.S. foreign policy.

The book presents a strategy for countering nuclear terrorism that embraces both technological and behavioral measures; it includes policies for deterrence and situation management on national and international scales and points toward a major reshaping of world order.

Louis René Beres, professor of political science and international law at Purdue University, has lectured and published extensively on the subjects of nuclear terrorism, nuclear strategy, and human rights. His works include *The Management of World Power: A Theoretical Analysis* (1973); *Reordering the Planet: Constructing Alternative World Futures* (with Harry R. Targ, 1974); *Transforming World Politics: The National Roots of World Peace* (1975); *Planning Alternative World Futures: Values, Methods and Models* (with Harry R. Targ, 1975); *Apocalypse: Nuclear Catastrophe in World Politics* (1980); *People, States and World Order* (1981); *Mimicking Sisyphus: America's Countervailing Nuclear Strategy* (1983); *Reason and Realpolitik: U.S. Foreign Policy and World Order* (1984); *Security or Armageddon: Israel's Nuclear Strategy* (1986); and *America Outside the World: The Collapse of U.S. Foreign Policy* (forthcoming).

Second Edition, Completely Revised and Updated

Terrorism and Global Security

The Nuclear Threat

Louis René Beres

Westview Press / Boulder and London

Westview Special Studies in National and International Terrorism

Copyright © 1987 by Westview Press, Inc.

Published in 1987 in the United States of America by Westview Press, Inc.; Frederick A. Praeger, Publisher; 5500 Central Avenue, Boulder, Colorado 80301

Library of Congress Cataloging-in-Publication Data
Beres, Louis René.
  Terrorism and global security.
  (Westview special studies in national and
international terrorism)
  Bibliography: p.
  Includes index.
  1. Terrorism. 2. Nuclear terrorism. I. Title.
II. Series.
HV6431.B47 1987   303.6'25   86-33952
ISBN 0-8133-0411-3

Printed and bound in the United States of America

The paper used in this publication meets the requirements of the American National Standard for Permanence of Paper for Printed Library Materials Z39.48-1984.

10   9   8   7   6   5   4   3   2   1

This book is dedicated to
all who would oppose the terrorizing reign of the herd
and who would refuse to transform despair into death

Contents

PART TWO
PREVENTING NUCLEAR TERRORISM

Preface

In the hazardous flux of world affairs, the specter of nuclear terrorism is particularly insidious. For the first time in humankind's history on this beleaguered planet, private *individuals* are capable of exploiting the destructive potential of nuclear technology. Understandably, fresh visions of oblivion and radioactive silence have kindled our apocalyptic imaginations, producing ever-greater levels of personal and collective insecurity. As if this were not frightful enough, those who might ultimately be confronted with responsibility for making crisis decisions concerning nuclear insurgency are frozen like the chorus in a Greek tragedy, distraught at the march of events that they feel powerless to control.

The situation *is* fraught with disquieting possibilities. But it is also too soon to despair. There are steps that can be taken, things that can and must be done, to prevent a new paradigm of violence. We need a plan, one that joins the elements of sound scholarship with the summoning and mastery of visions of atomic annihilation. With such a plan, we can begin to take the first critical steps back from a future that glows as a numbing hallucination.

The plan is complex. It cannot be limited to the sorts of "quick fix" physical security measures that are now in fashion. Rather, it must also include measures directed toward affecting the behavior of terrorists. And all strategies of counter–nuclear terrorism, technological and behavioral, need to be applied internationally.

Before we are able to finish our plan, we will understand its critical dependence upon a strengthened tapestry of international treaties and agreements directed at nonproliferation and superpower arms control. Moreover, because the success of counter–nuclear terrorism will require a major refashioning of the international legal order, we will explore the prospects for far-reaching transformations of foreign policy processes. In the final analysis, the prevention of nuclear terrorism will require states to move beyond the precarious dynamics of realpolitik to a new world politics of globalism. It would be futile to try to tinker with the portent of nuclear terrorism without such a change. *Planetization,* a new consciousness of unity and relatedness between states, is integral to all possibilities for enduring patterns of safety.

Louis René Beres

Acknowledgments

I am grateful to all of the people at Westview Press who encouraged me to prepare this book and who have taken a skillful part in its production or promotion: Miriam Gilbert, Susan L. McEachern, Karen Bordner, Janet L. Miller, Sandi Genova, Lauri Fults, and Beverly Armstrong. Sincere appreciation is also extended to Paul Leventhal, president of the Nuclear Control Institute, for allowing me to quote from the outstanding *Report of the International Task Force on Prevention of Nuclear Terrorism.* (This report, along with support studies, will be published in 1987.) Finally, I wish to thank Kim Orth of Purdue University's Department of Political Science for typing the manuscript with dispatch and good cheer.

L.R.B.

Acronyms

ABM	Antiballistic missile
ALF	Arab Liberation Front
ALN	Action for National Liberation
ASAT	antisatellite
BMD	ballistic missile defense
CEPS	Centre for European Policy Studies
CTB	comprehensive test ban
FLN	National Liberation Front
FLQ	Front de Liberation Quebecois
GNP	gross national product
IAEA	International Atomic Energy Agency
ICBM	intercontinental ballistic missile
IDA	Intrusion Detection Alarm
JRA	Japanese Red Army
MIRV	multiple independently targeted reentry vehicle
MOX	mixed oxides of uranium and plutonium
NAS	National Academy of Sciences
NATO	North Atlantic Treaty Organization
NEST	Nuclear Emergency Search Team
NNPA	Nuclear Non-Proliferation Act
NPT	Non-Proliferation Treaty
NRC	Nuclear Regulatory Commission
OPEC	Organization of Oil Producing and Exporting Countries

OTA	Office of Technology Assessment
PAL	Permissive Action Link
PDFLP	Popular Democratic Front for the Liberation of Palestine
PFLP	Popular Front for the Liberation of Palestine
PFLP-GC	Popular Front for the Liberation of Palestine–General Command
PLO	Palestine Liberation Organization
PRP	Personnel Reliability Program
RAD	Radiation Absorbed Dose
RBE	Radiation Biological Effectiveness
REM	Radiation Effective Man
SLBM	submarine-launched ballistic missile
SNM	special nuclear material
SSNM	strategic special nuclear material
USN	U.S. Navy

Terrorism and
Global Security

PART ONE

Understanding Nuclear Terrorism

1

The Specter of Nuclear Terrorism: An Overview

A Surrealist System: The Terrorist as Microcosm

The terrorist is a study in contradictions. Terrorists wish the birth of a certain kind of order, but in the delivery a gravedigger must wield the forceps. They wish to impress the world with the reasonableness of their claims but choose the tirade as their preferred means of communication. They stamp their predilections for violent excess with the imprimatur of innocence, yet it is only through the destruction of innocence that their aims can be realized.

How can we understand such contradictions? Even in the admittedly absurd theater of modern world politics, terrorists appear more than merely avant-garde. They seem genuinely pathological. Or is it, rather, the entire global human condition that is diseased, a disintegrating nonlandscape of irrationality in which only verbalized chaos remains truly comprehensible?

What is producing such contradictions? Is it an intangible but pervasive crisis of existential emptiness and despair from which human beings cannot escape? Is it the objectification of individuals into vast networks of social, economic, and political manipulation? Is it a fundamental disequilibrium that fractures the integrity of Earth's highly integrated system of cultural and biological adaptation? Or is it "simply" the failure to satisfy the diverse political hopes of unhappy people in unbearable circumstances?

Perhaps, in the Orwellian logic of our time, contradictions must be redefined altogether. Why should they offend our sense of correct reason? After all, we live in a world in which peace is sought through competition in strategic arms; in which the legal equality of states coexists with an institutionalized hierarchy of authority in the United Nations; and in which societies achieve high measures of growth through despoliation of their environments. In this world there is one soldier per forty-three

3

people, Nazi war criminals live almost everywhere undisturbed, and a former president of South Vietnam now runs a liquor store in California.

Against the backdrop of such a world, can the alleged contradictions of modern terrorism cause real consternation? Since George Orwell wrote the grim fantasy *1984,* his notion of "doublethink" has become a new orthodoxy of worldwide human relations. Understood as "the power of holding two contradictory beliefs in one's mind simultaneously, and accepting both of them," doublethink is now manifest not only in expressions of political propaganda, but also in the most widely revered documents of national and international law.

But not every instance of insurgency is an act of terrorism. Although specially constituted UN committees and the UN General Assembly have continually condemned acts of international terrorism,[1] they exempt those activities that derive from "the inalienable right to self-determination and independence of all peoples under colonial and racist regimes and other forms of alien domination and the legitimacy of their struggle, in particular the struggle of national liberation movements, in accordance with the purposes and principles of the Charter and the relevant resolutions of the organs of the United Nations." This exemption, from the 1973 General Assembly *Report of the Ad Hoc Committee on International Terrorism,*[2] is corroborated by Article 7 of the General Assembly's 1974 *Definition of Aggression.* According to Article 7:

> Nothing in this definition, and in particular Article 3 (inventory of acts that qualify as aggression[3]) could in any way prejudice the right to self-determination, freedom, and independence, as derived from the Charter, of peoples forcibly deprived of that right and referred to in the Declaration on Principles of International Law concerning Friendly Relations and Cooperation among States[4] in accordance with the Charter of the United Nations, particularly peoples under colonial and racist regimes or other forms of alien domination; nor the right of these peoples to struggle to that end and to seek and receive support, in accordance with the principles of the Charter and in conformity with the above-mentioned Declaration.[5]

International law has also approved certain forms of insurgency that are directed toward improving human rights where repression is neither colonial nor racist. Together with a number of important covenants, treaties, and declarations, the UN Charter codifies many binding norms on the protection of human rights. Comprising a human rights "regime," these rules of international law are effectively enforceable only by the actions of individual states or by lawful insurgencies.

International law, therefore, actually supports the legitimacy of certain forms of insurgency. Although this is important in light of the objectives of international justice, it does create severe problems in promoting the objectives of international order. The ultimate problem, of course, is allowing international law to serve the interests of order without impairing the legitimate interests of justice.

But how are we to determine the proper balance? And what criteria can be applied? Given the structure of a decentralized system of international law, individual states must bear the final responsibility for distinguishing between terrorism and lawful acts of insurgency.

What principles should inform their judgments? First, careful assessments must be made of particular regimes' conformance with the international law of human rights. Regime terror spawns revolutionary violence and must be opposed strenuously by the community of nations. Second, states must exhibit a deep and abiding concern for discrimination and proportionality in evaluating the legitimacy of insurgent uses of force. Once force is applied to any segment of human population, blurring the distinction between combatants and noncombatants, terrorism has surfaced. Similarly, once force is applied to the fullest possible extent, restrained only by the limits of available weaponry, terrorism is taking place.

The legitimacy of a certain cause does not legitimate the use of certain forms of violence. The ends do not justify the means. As in the case of war between states, every use of force by insurgents must be judged twice—once with regard to the justness of the objective, and once with regard to the justness of the means used in the fighting.

Facing the Gorgon Head: The Nature of Modern Terrorism

Today's terrorists are spurred on by a variety of motives. Some are moved by the wish to alter the devastating inequities of an unjust order. Here, there exists a long and venerable tradition. Where it is understood as resistance to despotism, terrorism has been countenanced and supported in the Bible and in the ancient and medieval classics. The tyrannicide motif can be found in Aristotle's *Politics,* Plutarch's *Lives,* and Cicero's *De Officiis.* According to Cicero:

> There can be no such thing as fellowship with tyrants, nothing but bitter feud is possible: and it is not repugnant to nature to despoil, if you can, those whom it is a virtue to kill; nay, this pestilent and godless brood should be utterly banished from human society. For, as we amputate a limb in which the blood and the vital spirit have ceased to circulate, because it injures the rest of the body, so monsters, who, under human guise, conceal the cruelty and ferocity of a wild beast, should be severed from the common body of humanity.[6]

Other terrorists, in the fashion of bandits, are moved by the selfish search for material gain. Still others, like the protagonist of André Malraux's *The Human Condition,* base their motive, consciously or unconsciously, on the need to escape from one form or another of private anguish. In this last category of motives, we discover the "incapacity for authentic relatedness" described in the various writings of Erich Fromm, the emptiness of T. S. Eliot's "hollow men," and the bottomless rage that is brought on by repeated and unrelenting doses of misfortune, a rage that produces the kinds of effects asserted by Shakespeare's Second Murderer in Act 2, Scene 1 of *Macbeth.*

I am one, my liege,
Whom the vile blows and buffets of the world,
Hath so incensed, that I am reckless what
I do to spite the world.

Occasionally, this combination of traits foments a genuinely psychopathic breed of terrorist, one who says, as Jerry Rubin once did, "When in doubt, burn," or one who feels, with Kozo Okamato, the surviving terrorist of the Lydda Airport massacre, "a strange ecstasy" in meting out death to innocents. Here, we are faced with the values of a Nechayev, the nineteenth-century Russian terrorist who served as one of the models for Dostoevsky's major figure in *The Possessed.* "He (the revolutionary) knows of only one science, the science of destruction. To this end, and this end alone, he will study mechanics, physics, chemistry, and perhaps medicine. To this end he will study day and night the living science: people, their characters and circumstances and all the features of the present social order at all possible levels. His sole and constant object is the immediate destruction of this vile order."[7]

One modern terrorist who explicitly identified himself with this "revolutionary catechism" is the founder of the Italian Red Brigades, Renato Curcio, who cited Nechayev with approval. "The revolutionary has neither personal business nor sentimental interests. He is without ties, property, or even a name. In the depth of his being, not only in words but in deeds, he has ruptured every tie with civil order and with all of the civilized world—with law, with custom, with morality, and those conventions generally recognized as of this world."[8]

In certain cases, today's terrorists display a need to move, to shock, to goad, to outrage, to reveal potency. Should such terrorists ever acquire the instruments of nuclear violence, the results may well include an unprecedented spasm of gratuitous killing and maiming. It would surely be a major mistake to conclude that such terrorists are incapable of wreaking profound unhappiness because of their condition. As Freud pointed out: "Fools, visionaries, sufferers from delusions, neurotics, and lunatics have played great roles at all times in the history of mankind, and not merely when the accident of birth had bequeathed them sovereignty. Usually, they have wreaked havoc." But we must not assume that only psychopathic terrorists are captivated by the romanticization of excessive violence. Al Fatah, the first Palestinian terrorist movement and precursor to the Arafat wing of the PLO (Palestine Liberation Organization), has articulated a doctrine of "liberation" through cataclysmic violence. Although such liberation is cast in terms of its unifying and purgative effects, it is also directed at a clear set of political/historical objectives.[9]

Origins and Regularities

Terrorism is not a recent phenomenon. It is older than the ancient civilizations of Greece and Rome. By manipulating fear in a special way, terrorists have been able to affect political behavior in a fashion totally disproportionate to their numbers.[10]

In the political realm, fear produces intimidation when it issues from the threat of violence. It is not necessary to modify this statement by speaking exclusively of arbitrary or indiscriminate violence, as these characteristics are an irremediable part of the definition. All violence, as Hannah Arendt has reminded us, is unpredictable.[11] Unlike power, force, or strength, violence is always applied with unforeseeable effects. The ensuing domination by *Fortuna,* or fate, creates a devastating aura of uncertainty, one in which the hegemony of means over ends may paralyze the will of potential opponents. As a result, terrorism is consecrated as an "improvement" upon war as the ultima ratio in world affairs, a strategy whereby the weak become effectual participants on the global stage.

Since the close of the eighteenth century, we have had a great many instances and forms of terrorism. In view of this heterogeneity, are there any ascertainable regularities, common features concerning characteristics and composition that are essential to theorizing about terrorism? Looking over the current landscape of operational groups, we find anarchists, separatists, Marxist-Leninists, reactionaries, and every conceivable brand of anti-imperialist and national liberationist. Their intellectual and spiritual mentors include a gallery of heroes featuring Bakhunin, Marx, Lenin, Trotsky,[12] Sorel, Marighella, Mao, Giap, Fanon, Marcuse, Malcolm X, Guevara, Debray, and Guillen. What could this tangled skein of programs and participants possibly have in common?

This question seems even more problematic when we consider the fragmentation and factionalization within particular groups and movements. Nonetheless, these strange bedfellows have sometimes identified enough commonality to cooperate across geographic and ideological lines. What do these cooperative terrorist ventures suggest? A single "terrorist mind" that, if properly understood, will produce effective strategies of counterterrorism? By no means! Attempts have been made to create a "profile of terrorists." Such attempts do not contradict the fundamental heterogeneity of the subject, but they have illuminated some interesting commonalities. Admittedly intriguing, such profiles have not significantly advanced the search for essential theory. After all, the identification of common characteristics regarding age, sex, marital status, rural versus urban origin, social and economic background, education or occupation, method or place of recruitment, and political-economic philosophy does not lead to the sort of behavioral strategy that can reduce the likelihood of nuclear terrorism. To create such a strategy we need to ask different questions, ones that explore far more crucial variables than those selected by the profilers.

What are these different questions? They are questions that are intended to produce a fuller understanding of the risk calculations of terrorists. Hence, they focus upon those variables that are most likely to affect such calculations. Until we understand the special terrorist stance on the balance of risks that can be taken in world politics, and the vital differences between terrorist groups on this stance, we will not be able to identify an appropriate system of sanctions. To properly understand the decisional calculi of terrorist groups, we must first come to grips with the following questions, as we intend to do throughout this study.

1. Is there a particular ordering of preferences that is common to many or all terrorists groups, or is there significant variation from one group to another? If it can be determined that many or all terrorist groups actually share a basic hierarchy of wants, a general strategy of counter-nuclear-terrorist operations can begin to be shaped. Alternatively, if significant variation in preference orderings can be detected between terrorist groups, myriad strategies of an individually tailored nature will have to be identified.

2. Are there particular preferences that tend to occupy the highest positions in the preference hierarchies of terrorist groups, and how might these preferences be effectively obstructed? In this connection, it is especially important to examine the widely held assumption that terrorists, like states, are most anxious to avoid negative physical sanctions. In fact, a great deal of sophisticated conceptual analysis and experimental evidence appears to indicate that such sanctions are apt to be ineffective in limiting aggression and may actually prove counterproductive.

3. To what extent, if any, would the obstruction of terrorist preferences prove offensive to some of the principal values of states? In this case,

we must be concerned about the very real possibility that effective counter-nuclear-terrorist measures might be injurious to such values as social justice and human rights within particular states. Here, states must first decide whether the prospective benefits of proposed antiterrorist activity are great enough to outweigh the prospective costs to major segments of their own populations.

4. To what extent, if any, are the risk calculations of terrorist actors affected by geographic dispersion and intermingling with state actors? Because terrorists do not occupy a piece of territory in the manner of states, they are not susceptible to orthodox threats of deterrence. How, then, might effective counter-nuclear-terrorist efforts be reconciled with the reality of geographic dispersion?

5. To what extent, if any, might the decisional calculi of terrorist actors be receptive to positive cues or sanctions as opposed to negative ones, and exactly what rewards seem to warrant consideration? In this connection, special attention might be directed to studies of child rearing, which indicate with overwhelming regularity that positive sanctions (rewards) are generally far more effective than negative ones (punishment).

6. To what extent would the implementation of effective counter-nuclear-terrorist measures require special patterns of international cooperation, and how might such patterns be created? In principle, the surest path to success in averting nuclear terrorism lies in a unified opposition to terrorist activity by states; yet, at least in the immediate future, this kind of opposition is assuredly not forthcoming. We must, therefore, ask ourselves what cooperative patterns between *particular* states can cope with the problem.

7. To what extent, if any, are the risk calculations of terrorists affected by their relations with "host" states? Because terrorist actors necessarily operate within the framework of individual states, the character of the relationship between "visitor" and "host" may affect the viability of counter-nuclear-terrorist measures. How, therefore, might we exploit what is known about such relationships in curbing the threat of nuclear terrorism?

8. To what extent, if any, are the risk calculations of terrorist actors affected by alignments with state actors or with other terrorist groups? And how, therefore, can we use what we know about such effects to devise an effective counter-nuclear-terrorist strategy?

9. To what extent, if any, are the risk calculations of terrorist actors affected by the terrorist pattern of random and uninhibited violence? In asking this particular question, we treat terrorist orientations to violence as an independent variable in order to treat it more effectively as a dependent variable later on.

10. To what extent, if any, are the risk calculations of terrorist actors affected by the degree to which their policies evoke sympathy and support from others? As almost all acts of terror are essentially propagandistic, it is important to understand their desired effects on selected publics in order to prevent escalation to a nuclear option.

By considering these basic questions, students of nuclear terrorism can create the foundations of a genuinely auspicious behavioral strategy. With such a strategy in hand, steps can be taken to create inhibitions in the use of violence by terrorists and to impede the growing cooperation of terrorist groups. As with all other groups of human beings, terrorists acquire a repertoire of behavior under the particular contingencies of reinforcement to which they are exposed. The "trick" is to understand this repertoire and to use it to inform the differential reinforcement of alternative courses of action. Once this is done, the specter of nuclear terrorism can be confronted with countermeasures that are grounded in a coherent profile of variables likely to affect terrorist actions. Such a profile is logically antecedent to successful strategies of deterrence and situation management.

The U.S. Imperative

Before the United States can reduce the risk of nuclear terrorism, however, its leaders must also understand the differences between lawful and unlawful insurgencies. And this understanding must be based upon more than the desolate intuitions of geopolitics. Specifically, it must rest upon well-established jurisprudential standards that reflect not only international law but also the most cherished elements of U.S. political tradition.

The Declaration of Independence sets limits on the authority of every government. Because justice, according to the Founding Fathers, must bind all human society, the rights articulated by the declaration cannot be reserved only to Americans. To deny these rights to others on narrow political grounds is illogical and self-contradictory, as it undermines the permanent and universal Law of Nature from which the Declaration of Independence derives. Indeed, this idea was reaffirmed on February 22, 1985, by Secretary of State George Shultz in an address titled "America and the Struggle for Freedom": "All Americans can be proud that the example of our Founding Fathers has helped to inspire millions around the globe. Throughout our own history, we have always believed that freedom is the birthright of all peoples and that we could not be true to ourselves or our principles unless we stood for freedom and democracy not only for ourselves but for others."[13] In this nation's early years, George Washington noted, in his Farewell Address, "The foundations of our national policy must be laid in the pure and immutable principles of private morality." Accepting the wisdom of our first president, this country must change direction before it is too late. Although it is both correct and pragmatic to oppose terrorism in every form, we must first acknowledge a lawful definition of terrorism.

Today, the Reagan administration embraces only one standard of judgment concerning U.S. foreign policy: anti-Sovietism. Human rights have nothing to do with this standard. It follows that efforts to overthrow allegedly pro-Soviet regimes are always conducted by "freedom fighters" (even where these efforts involve rape, pillage, and mass murder) whereas efforts to oppose anti-Soviet regimes (even where these efforts are undertaken by the most oppressed and downtrodden peoples of genocidal regimes) are always conducted by "terrorists." Consider President Reagan's statement, at a press conference on March 21, 1985, that the seventeen blacks that had recently been shot by South African police were not "simply killed," but were the excusable casualties of "rioting." Moments later, reacting to a question about Nicaragua, the president defended the use of force against a "Communist tyranny." In other words, rebellion against apartheid[14] must always be peaceful, but opposition to Sandinista rule must always be violent.

With this view, black South Africans, although understandably unhappy to be victims of a uniquely repressive regime, were instructed to be "patient" as the United States continued with its policy of "constructive engagement." At the same time, contra rebels—widely and authoritatively associated with the execution of noncombatants in Nicaragua and with death-squad activities in El Salvador and Honduras—were embraced by the president as "our brothers." These "freedom fighters," said the president to reporters on March 1, "are the moral equal of our Founding Fathers."

The Reagan administration bases its selective regard for human rights on pure bravado. As a result, many of the world's peoples now see this country as an affliction, and insurgent groups throughout the world are likely to accelerate their activities against the United States. In others words, by its failure to recognize the connection between regime terror and insurgent terror, the United States will render itself increasingly vulnerable to terrorism in general and to nuclear terrorism in particular.

The Reagan administration's tolerance of repression in "authoritarian" regimes is not the only cause of this increasing vulnerability; another cause is active U.S. opposition to certain "totalitarian" governments. In Nicaragua, for example, it is obvious that the contras—even with significant levels of U.S. aid—will be defeated. An expected consequence of this defeat—in addition to hardened anti-U.S. resolve by the Sandinista regime—may well be terrorism directed against the United States and/

or its interests and personnel abroad. The origins of this terrorism might lie not only with the Sandinistas, who will have been pushed into the arms of the Soviet Union by self-defeating U.S. policies, but also with the remnants of an embittered contra force.

There has been no learning from lessons of the past. What can the Reagan administration hope to accomplish by standing alongside such pariah states as Chile and South Africa while unleashing attacks against less repressive regimes? If we are really interested in protecting ourselves against terrorism, why do we persist in support of governments that make terrorism inevitable? If we fear that Chile will become "another Nicaragua," why did we install the Pinochet regime in the first place? And if we fear that Nicaragua will become "another Cuba," why do we cling foolishly to interventionist policies that leave the Sandinistas no other choice?

Current policies that spawn terrorism against the United States also ensure the opposition of governments-in-the-making. During the next few years, insurgents fighting against U.S.-supported regime terror in such places as Chile, Paraguay, and South Africa will likely prevail. Installed with authority, these former rebels will—in the fashion of Cuba, Nicaragua, and Iran—become enemies of the United States. Sadly, this development will have been avoidable if only this country had remained true to its doctrinal foundations, opposing not only "leftist thugs" (President Reagan's characterization to reporters of the regime overthrown in Grenada) but all tyrannical regimes (that is, rightist thugs as well).

What will happen when the opponents of U.S.-supported repression in Latin America and South Africa mount successful insurgencies, creating successor governments with strongly anti-U.S. leanings? The answer is entirely predictable. The United States will begin the next phase of geopolitical competition, mounting its own insurgencies to topple regimes that are now left wing. Resembling the administration's current war against Nicaragua, these insurgencies—conducted by "freedom fighters"—will seek to bring down a black majority government in South Africa that will be denounced as a "Soviet pawn." By this reasoning, the present condition of apartheid (as with Somoza's rule in Nicaragua) may be described as the "lesser evil."

The principal danger of terrorism lies not in the guerrilla camps of Central America and southern Africa. The enemy lies in ourselves. By supporting invidious regimes in pursuit of anti-Soviet advantage, we spark and sustain a worldwide insurgency against the United States. Our mistake is always the same. Failing to understand that revolutionary movements are often caused by long-established patterns of repression, we localize all evil in the Soviet Union. Hence we continue to act against our own interests, sustaining a condition of enmity that elicits terrorism against the United States. In the words of Octavio Paz, the Mexican poet and essayist, in a 1982 article titled "Latin America and Democracy":

> . . . the revolts and agitations that are unsettling our continent, especially Central America, are not the result of a Russo-Cuban conspiracy, nor of the machinations of international communism, as US government spokesmen keep repeating. We all know that these movements have been caused by the social injustices, poverty and lack of public freedoms that are prevalent in many Latin American countries. The Soviets did not invent discontent; they merely use it and try to subvert it to their own ends. We must admit that they almost always succeed. The errant policies of the United States have had something to do with this result.[15]

Curiously, the United States, founded upon the principles of revolution, has become the archetype of counterrevolution. Guided by shortsighted economic considerations and shallow politics, the United States is perceived to have propped up oligarchies, spawned militarism, and thwarted hesitant national struggles to enter the modern world. According to Octavio Paz: "This is tragic because American democracy inspired the fathers of our Independence and our great liberals like Sarmiento and Juarez. From the 18th century onward, for us modernization has meant democracy and free institutions: and the archetype of this political and social modernity was United States democracy. History's nemesis: in Latin America the United States has been the protector of tyrants and the ally of democracy's enemies."[16]

In the final analysis, U.S. safety from terrorism will depend largely upon its ability to disengage from an all-consuming anti-Sovietism. In making anti-Sovietism the centerpiece of its foreign policy, the United States adopts an orientation to global affairs that encourages terrorism. The best way to counter terrorism is not the childlike muscle-flexing of military power, but a renewed commitment to decency and justice in global affairs. Restored to our capacity to bear witness as a righteous people, we could progress beyond the desolate clichés of cold war posturing to improved safety from terrorist attack.

From the point of view of the United States, there is one immediate imperative: to end the singular U.S. preoccupation with cold war theology. By casting every issue of foreign policy within the limiting context of Soviet-U.S. competition, the United States endorses an inscrutable logic whereby many of the most repressive regimes are included in the free world, and according to which U.S. military intervention on behalf of "freedom" becomes self-justifying. As a result, the victims of regime terror and of U.S. interference with self-determination identify the United

States as their enemy, a tragic and humiliating association that ensures U.S. vulnerability to insurgent terror.

In *The Plague,* Camus tells us: "At the beginning of the pestilence and when it ends, there's always a propensity for rhetoric. . . . It is in the thick of a calamity that one gets hardened to the truth—in other words, to silence." As long as the United States continues to stand in the ruins of thought, ruins created by its frenzied and perpetual enmity with the Soviet Union, it will be unable to avoid the more tangible ruins of terrorism. And if there is no progress beyond the facile tenets of realpolitik, these ruins might well be generated by nuclear explosives or radioactivity.

Yet, current U.S. foreign policy is not the only source of possible nuclear terrorism against the United States. Even if a dramatic transformation of current policy orientations were to occur, a significant hazard would remain. To reduce this hazard, major improvements are needed in preventing terrorist access to assembled nuclear weapons, nuclear power plants, and nuclear-waste storage facilities. Included in these improvements must be measures to contain the spread of nuclear weapons to additional countries.

2

The Etiology of Nuclear Terrorism

It is now widely understood that terrorist access to weapons of mass destruction represents the single most substantial portent of nuclear terrorism. However, such access assumes serious dimensions only when coupled with four additional conditions: terrorist orientations to nuclear violence, terrorist insensitivity to traditional threats of deterrence, cooperation between terrorist groups, and tolerance and support of terrorism. In this chapter, we will explore these five factors, which—taken together—give rise to an unprecedented hazard.[1]

Terrorist Access to Nuclear Weapons

In a century wherein humankind has learned to stoke the crematory fires with enthusiasm, nothing can give greater cause for alarm than the access of terrorists to nuclear weapons, nuclear power plants, or nuclear-waste storage facilities. Yet, considerable evidence now suggests that determined terrorist groups might acquire nuclear weapons via the theft of assembled systems from military stockpiles or by self-development from pilfered weapons-grade nuclear material. It is also widely recognized that terrorists might attempt to sabotage nuclear reactors.

To acquire an assembled weapon, terrorist operatives might aim at any of the tens of thousands of nuclear weapons now deployed in the national or alliance arsenals of the United States, the Soviet Union, France, England, India, and China. Such terrorists are likely to have an enlarged arena of opportunity in the future. This is because the number of states possessing nuclear weapons may grow and because new members of the nuclear club are apt to waive essential safeguards.

According to the *Report of the International Task Force on Prevention of Nuclear Terrorism,* a special problem area lies in the widespread deployment of tactical nuclear weapons:

There have been published reports of one terrorist group in Europe having tried unsuccessfully to obtain information on NATO nuclear-weapon storage

facilities, and of another having sought unsuccessfully to enlist the help
of a nuclear scientist regarding nuclear weapons they considered stealing.
One national leader, regarded as being engaged in sponsoring terrorism,
is reported to have sought unsuccessfully to buy nuclear weapons while
pursuing a nuclear research program that could be applied in the long
term to making bombs.[2]

Moreover, the report noted that it is not enough to keep terrorists from
assembled nuclear weapons. Efforts must also be undertaken to equip
individual weapons with safety locking devices. With the most advanced
self-protecting systems in place, nuclear weapons would be useless to
terrorists who had managed to acquire them.

U.S. nuclear weapons in Europe—now reduced to about 4,800—are
protected, inter alia, by Permissive Action Link (PAL) mechanisms,
locking devices to prevent unauthorized use. But U.S. Navy weapons,
including submarine missiles and tactical weapons, do not have PALs,
at least on board ship. It follows, as the task force report noted, that
"Navy tactical weapons are vulnerable to use by terrorists if successfully
seized."[3]

To combat terrorism by military means, the United States has created
the Delta Forces and has also created the Special Operations Forces for
a multitude of tasks. The army is currently forming new light divisions;
the marines are developing new capabilities; and the air force and army
are developing new concepts and doctrines.[4] But how effective can these
forces be in protecting U.S. and NATO nuclear weapons from terrorist
diversion? According to Rear Admiral Thomas Davies (USN, retired):

> In theory, nuclear weapons should be consistently secured by the highest
> quality systems and personnel. One suspects, however, that the military
> community includes a normal spectrum of good and bad, some ineptitude,
> and the vagaries of administration characteristic of an excessively large
> bureaucracy. How well does military security protect against terrorism?
> The Beirut attacks confirm that it was not then designed with terrorism
> in mind.[5]

To safeguard nuclear weapons in other countries, the task force report
suggested the development of new national NESTs—Nuclear Emergency
Search Teams. Operated in the United States by the Department of
Energy, NEST represents a small, highly skilled unit that can respond
to threats of nuclear terrorism. In the final analysis, improved worldwide
security for nuclear weapons may require establishment of an international
NEST, fully authorized to request assistance in the form of technical
resources of the nuclear-weapons states.[6]

In principle, nuclear terrorism might even exploit weapons under Soviet control, but that is far less likely. As Bernard J. O'Keefe, chairman of EG&G, Inc. (a company involved in development, testing, and protection of nuclear weapons), testified recently before the House Committee on Foreign Affairs, Subcommittee on International Security and Scientific Affairs, "It is true that the Soviets condone and probably encourage conventional terrorist activities, but under no conditions have they or will they knowingly permit a nuclear explosive to get out of their tight control, not even to their Warsaw Pact allies."[7]

Self-Development of Nuclear Weapons

To manufacture their own nuclear weapons, terrorists would require both strategic special nuclear materials (SSNM) and the expertise to convert them into bombs or radiological weapons. As is now widely revealed, both requirements are well within the range of terrorist capabilities. According to Rear Admiral Davies:

. . . theft of nuclear explosive materials has to be considered a serious threat. In attempting to gauge its likelihood, we must first acknowledge that we don't know how much, if any, may already have been stolen. There is too much of it unaccounted for: In the U.S. alone, at least nine thousand pounds was missing from the books through 1981. . . . Some 260 commercial nuclear power plants are operating in the non-Communist world today. Each has the capacity to produce bomb-capable plutonium, some up to 300 kilograms a year—all together a total of about 45 metric tons a year, the equivalent of at least 6,000 nuclear weapons. Approximately twenty plants, in seventeen countries, can now process plutonium from reactor spent fuel. Current economic and political problems with the plutonium fuel cycle and breeders make it difficult to estimate accurately how much plutonium will be in circulation by the year 2000. Earlier estimates have been scaled down to about 400 tons—still an awesome quantity: nearly twice the combined weapons stockpiles of plutonium held by the superpowers today. It is projected that the amount of civilian plutonium in the world will exceed the superpowers' military stocks within the next decade. The once super-secret technology of uranium enrichment, which produces fuel for reactors and material for weapons, is also proliferating. Worldwide, at least 12 countries are known to have enrichment facilities. As the quantities of these explosive materials follow a constant upward curve, they are always traveling—moving by air, sea, truck, and railway from the mines to the enrichment plants, the fabricators, bomb assembly depots, power reactors, processing plants, and storage. Transport of so much dangerous material in open commerce may well turn out to be the Achilles heel of the nuclear industry, a prime target for terrorist theft.[8]

Such fears have been echoed by Congressman Ron Wyden, speaking before the Subcommittee on International Security:

> In a recent letter from Energy and Commerce Committee Chairman John Dingell to Secretary of Energy Don Hodel, which was printed in the October 27 Congressional Record of this year (1984), Chairman Dingell also expresses grave concern about the extremely lax security measures of the Department of Energy in safeguarding nuclear facilities. According to that letter, past reviews of the security in force at these facilities have uncovered unguarded quantities of plutonium, guards who could not shoot, and guards who responded to security drills 16 minutes after the mock attackers had left with the plutonium.[9]

Both the U.S. Department of Energy and the U.S. Nuclear Regulatory Commission (NRC) have developed threat models for the design of effective physical protection systems. Significantly, however, the models were designed a decade ago, at a time when the threat of nuclear terrorism was substantially less formidable. Thus, the NRC's "design basis threat" allegedly does not require protection at a reactor against more than one insider working with "several" outsiders.[10]

The Department of Energy maintains its own protective system criteria, but security standards seem inconsistent. According to the *Report of the International Task Force on Prevention of Nuclear Terrorism,* a 1984 congressional investigation of specific instances of physical security problems at U.S. nuclear-weapon facilities disclosed the following:

> ". . . nuclear test devices highly vulnerable to theft"; attitudinal problems and administrators who have covered up security problems; guard forces with less than 1 percent chance of interrupting an attacking force; "major deficiencies" in the management of the physical protection program; and, in the words of the chairman of the investigating committee, evidence that key officials "had put this nation's national security and public health and safety in serious jeopardy." Substantial improvements in physical protection have been made at these facilities since the disclosures were made.[11]

It also appears that nuclear security under the auspices of the U.S. Department of Defense is greater than that supplied by the Department of Energy. Although the Pentagon has developed equipment to provide electronic detection of an adversary force long before it reaches the perimeter fences of its nuclear-weapon installations, there is allegedly no parallel requirement at the Department of Energy nuclear-weapon facilities. At these facilities, it seems the requirement is for detection by humans beyond the perimeter fence. As a result, the International Task

Force on Prevention of Nuclear Terrorism recommended that "consideration should be given to use of DoD research and equipment, such as foliage-penetrating radar."[12]

All of these insights into the availability of nuclear materials are disturbing. Yet, it is even more disturbing to recognize that the removal of U.S. deficiencies might have no significant effect upon the prospect of nuclear-materials theft. This is because the protection of strategic special nuclear materials, as in the case of assembled nuclear weapons, must be effective on a worldwide basis. U.S. safeguards cannot secure against nuclear weapons fashioned from nuclear materials stolen elsewhere.[13]

Regrettably, the amount of nuclear materials present in other countries could expand. Pilot reprocessing plants to extract weapons-usable plutonium from spent reactor-fuel rods signal dangerous conditions. Unless immediate and effective steps are taken to inhibit the spread of plutonium reprocessing and uranium enrichment facilities to other countries, terrorist opportunities to acquire fissonable materials for nuclear-weapons purposes could reach very high levels.[14]

There are good reasons for reexamining the widespread commercial use of plutonium. Reserves of non-weapon-usable nuclear fuels are high and readily available at low prices. A decisive shift toward such fuels could permit storage or disposal of spent fuel without reprocessing— the so-called "once-through" fuel cycle.[15] About forty-five tons of plutonium are being discharged each year as waste in the spent fuel of commercial nuclear power plants. By the year 2000 a total of some 1,400 tons of plutonium will have been produced in spent fuel.[16] Initially many countries sought to reprocess plutonium to provide startup cores for plutonium breeder reactors. However, projections of nuclear power growth no longer remain high, and low-cost uranium resources no longer seem scarce. Hence, as nuclear experts Harold A. Feiveson, Frank von Hippel, and David Albright pointed out, "Programs to commercialize the breeder reactor are therefore grinding to a halt all over the world, and it is clear that the startup cores of the few demonstration breeder reactors which will be completed will not absorb a significant fraction of the world's rapidly growing accumulation of separated plutonium."[17]

To manufacture its own nuclear weapons, a terrorist group would also require expertise. It is now well known that such expertise is widely available. In 1977, the Office of Technology Assessment (OTA) produced a report entitled *Nuclear Proliferation and Safeguards*. After a general description of the two basic methods of assembling fissile material in a nuclear explosive (the assembly of two or more subcritical masses using gun propellants and the achievement of supercriticality of fissile material via high explosive), the report stated that "militarily useful weapons with reliable nuclear yields in the kiloton range can be constructed with reactor-grade plutonium, using low technology." Moreover, "given the weapons material and a fraction of a million dollars, a small group of people, none of whom had ever had access to the classified literature, could possibly design and build a crude nuclear explosive device."[18]

Approximately three years before the OTA report, a book by Mason Willrich and Theodore Taylor opened the eyes of policymakers and informed citizens. According to the authors, "The design and manufacture of a crude nuclear explosive is no longer a difficult task technically, and a plutonium dispersal device which can cause widespread radioactive contamination is much simpler to make than an explosive."[19] On March 22, 1978, in a statement presented to the Senate Committee on Governmental Affairs, Dr. Taylor elaborated on his views:

> Given the required amounts of special nuclear materials (plutonium, highly enriched uranium, uranium-233, or any other heavy elements from which fission explosives can be made without having to perform isotope enrichment), in a variety of chemical and physical forms, it is highly credible that a small group of people could design and build fission explosives, using information and non-nuclear materials that are accessible to the public worldwide. Under some circumstances, it is quite conceivable that this could be done by one person working alone. Such explosives could be transported by automobile. Their probable explosive yields would depend considerably on the knowledge and skills of the group. Relatively crude explosives that would be likely to yield the equivalent of up to about 1000 tons of high explosive would be much easier to build than explosives that could be reliably expected to yield the equivalent of more than 10 kilotons of high explosive. Explosives with yields in the latter range would be much easier to build with highly enriched uranium or uranium-233 than with plutonium. All three materials, including plutonium of all isotopic compositions could be used for making relatively crude explosives with yields in the vicinity of one kiloton.[20]

For several years, Taylor's views concerning terrorist fabrication of nuclear explosives had been challenged by others. In most cases, Taylor's acquaintance with classified information made it impossible for him to respond to these challenges satisfactorily. However, on March 15, 1978, he was shown a draft manuscript on the design and manufacture of nuclear weapons, written by Dimitri Rotow, an undergraduate student. This manuscript, entitled "Nuclear Weapons Design and Construction," was written without expert assistance of any kind and without access to classified national security information or restricted data. Commenting on these efforts of a twenty-two-year-old student, Dr. Taylor testified:

Mr. Rotow's manuscript is the most extensive and detailed exposition that I have seen outside the classified literature. Although it contains a number of errors, these do not generally detract from his main lines of reasoning in setting down a variety of approaches to the design of a variety of types of fission weapons. I was astonished by the amount of well-organized information and the number and quality of ideas he was able to assemble in a time that he says was about three months of intensive work. I would say his exposition is much stronger in dealing with design principles, and the reasoning behind them, than on estimates of performance, in which I found significant errors. All in all, however, I was neither shocked nor surprised that an intelligent and innovative person without extensive training in nuclear physics could produce such a document, though I was surprised that it took so little time. His work certainly tends to confirm a conviction I have held for more than 12 years.[21]

Rotow's work was not the first to underscore the credibility of the Taylor argument. That distinction belongs to a twenty-year-old Massachusetts Institute of Technology undergraduate who created an accurate technical design for a fission explosive that was documented in the "Nova" science series on public television on March 9, 1975. Later, a much more widely publicized case involved a twenty-one-year-old physics major at Princeton University, who designed an atomic bomb in four months with information obtained entirely from public documents. The point of his design, said John Aristotle Phillips, who later wrote a best-selling book on the affair, "was to show that any undergraduate with a physics background can do it, and therefore that it is reasonable to assume that terrorists could do it too."[22]

Less widely recognized, but similarly worth considering, are the cases of two small U.S. journals that printed articles on building atomic bombs, as well as the "bomb class" at a student-run experimental college. Articles in both the underground newspaper *Take Over* and the feminist journal *Majority Report* contained detailed plans on how to build an atomic bomb using a coffee can and explosives. The article in *Take Over* (published in the July 4, 1974, issue) was adapted by the feminist journal with the title, "Handy Woman's Guide: How to Build Your Own Atomic Bomb and Strike a Balance of Power with the Patriarchy."[23] A course entitled "How to Build an Atomic Bomb" was introduced at the University of Connecticut's Experimental College in the Fall 1977 semester. Its purpose, according to the college's handbook, was "to draw attention to the dangers of nuclear power." By demonstrating the "comparative ease with which an atomic bomb can be made," the course hoped to demonstrate the dangers of nuclear terrorism.[24]

All of the foregoing cases involved fission explosives. The clandestine manufacture of a pure fusion explosive (a device that would not require any fission "trigger" to initiate explosive thermonuclear reactions in very light hydrogen isotopes such as deuterium and tritium) is another matter entirely. Such explosives require very sophisticated equipment, exceptionally skilled and experienced experts, and large sums of money. With these facts in mind, the case involving *Progressive* magazine's blocked attempt to publish an article entitled "How a Hydrogen Bomb Works" may be viewed in a more rational perspective.

This case, which broke to the public in March 1979, concerned an article written by a thirty-six-year-old freelance writer with little scientific experience. Moreover, the article was written without the benefit of classified materials. Apart from the esoteric questions of constitutionality that were involved in this matter, it is exceedingly unlikely that such an article would have benefitted aspiring nuclear terrorists. Indeed, the extraordinary difficulties that would be entailed in fusion terrorism were identified by Dimitri Rotow in Senate testimony:

> I think it is highly unlikely that any terrorist group would ever have the technical sophistication to actually produce a thermonuclear device. I have made several runthroughs at designing thermonuclear triggers and discovered that, in my understanding of the particular configuration the Government used to produce efficient triggers to detonate a thermonuclear device, it is a rather difficult thing to do, both to calculate it out and to actually build it. Building the thermonuclear part of the bomb, in any event, would involve terrorists diverting quantities of tritium and several other exotic isotopes of hydrogen and lithium. So I don't think that is rather likely, although I feel absolutely certain that a team of two physicists or perhaps even a single physicist, a nuclear engineer, could go through the existing literature in a period of less than 6 months and by reviewing all of the data on fusion research or power plant design come up with quite an accurate and convincing design for thermonuclear weapons. There is the concern that such a device would cost an incredible amount to build. My first try at such a design resulted in something that would easily cost several million dollars and would be about the size of a railroad tank car.[25]

Nevertheless, terrorist fabrication of a small but very destructive fission device is clearly plausible. In the words of the task force report:

> . . . building a crude nuclear device, although more difficult than previously suggested by some experts, is within reach of terrorists having sufficient resources to recruit a team of three or four technically qualified specialists. The team need not have previous experience in building weapons, but would need chemical high explosives and a sufficient quantity of weapon-usable nuclear material, most probably in metallic form. A special study

prepared for the Task Force by a team of former U.S. weapons designers has established that crude nuclear bomb-making, while not as simple as once supposed, can be accomplished with a sufficient quantity of reactor-grade plutonium (the kind separated by industry in some countries from the spent fuel of a power reactor) or highly enriched uranium (the kind used to fuel many research rectors) in metallic or possibly even in oxide form.[26]

Sabotage of Nuclear Reactors

Another path to nuclear capability by terrorists might involve the sabotage of nuclear reactor facilities. It is now apparent that such acts could pose monumental problems for responsible government authorities. This is especially apparent in the aftermath of the Soviet nuclear accident at Chernobyl in the spring of 1986. Although a great many steps appear to have been taken in the United States during the past few years to diminish the vulnerability of nuclear power plants, sabotage is certainly conceivable.[27] Consider the following scenario of nuclear plant sabotage:

The twin plants of the Calvert Cliffs Nuclear Power station are sited in a park-like setting overlooking a river in southern Maryland, 50 miles from Washington, D.C. There is a fence surrounding the plant area, and a guard at the gate. But immediately adjacent and slightly above the enclosed area are attractively landscaped parking and picnic facilities provided by the company for tourists who come to see the plants. There are 10 or 15 cars parked on this afternoon, plus a couple of school buses and a somewhat oversized van—apparently outsized to house both people and audio equipment of a roving rock band. At some point the members of the rock group announce they are taking their picnic below the cliffs to the water's edge. Forty minutes later a tremendous explosion is heard at Solomon's Island, twenty miles down the road. The power station is rubble. One of the plants was operating at the time of the blast. Radiation greater than that produced by a nuclear weapon is released on the countryside, and drifts toward Washington.[28]

This scenario, offered by Thomas Davies, is certainly plausible. According to a recent study of the effects of conventional explosives against nuclear facilities by the Sandia National Laboratories, "unacceptable damage to vital reactor systems could occur from a relatively small charge at close distances and also from larger but still reasonable size charges at large setback distances (greater than the protected area for most plants)."[29]

Accordingly, the *Report of the International Task Force on Prevention of Nuclear Terrorism* offered the following short-term recommendations for the protection of nuclear facilities:

1. Denial of access to nuclear facilities should be the basic consideration in protecting against sabotage.
2. Thorough vigilance against the insider threat is needed.
3. Guard forces should be thoroughly trained and authorized to use deadly force.
4. The basis used for designing physical protection of nuclear plants should be reviewed to ensure that it accurately reflects the current threat.
5. Power reactors should be protected against vehicular threats.
6. Research reactors should have adequate security provisions against terrorists.
7. Reactor safety designs should be reexamined to protect against an accident caused by terrorists.
8. IAEA (International Atomic Energy Agency) physical protection guidelines should be reviewed and updated.
9. Protection standards should be spelled out unambiguously.[30]

Terrorist Inclinations to Nuclear Violence

Observing the behavior of modern terrorists, we may be reminded of the world described in William Butler Yeats's poem "The Second Coming," a world in which "the worst are full of passionate intensity, while the best lack all conviction." Displaying an orientation to violence that has been shockingly indiscriminate, many of today's terrorist groups have abandoned the idea of distinguishing between combatants and noncombatants.[31] As a result of this calculus, terrorist activities have occasioned the killing and maiming of many innocent people.

The unwillingness to create boundaries in the threat and use of violence—an unwillingness that suggests a serious likelihood of nuclear terrorism should access to nuclear weapons or nuclear power plants be afforded insurgent groups—is the essence of terrorism. The mere threat or use of force for political ends does not signify the operation of terrorism. It is necessary that such force be threatened or applied *indiscriminately.*

Ironically, this meaning of terrorism was perhaps better understood by Aristotle than by most modern political scientists. Writing about the species of fear that arises from tragedy, Aristotle emphasized that such fear "demands a person who suffers undeservedly" and that it must be felt by "one of ourselves." This fear, or terror, has nothing to do with our concern for an impending misfortune to others, but from our perceived resemblance to the victim. We feel terror on our own behalf;

we fear that *we* may become the objects of commiseration. Terror, in short, is fear referred back to ourselves.

Of course, Aristotle's *Poetics* does not deal with political terrorism, and the feelings of theatrical catharsis bear no direct resemblance to the sentiments of modern observers of terrorist violence. Yet, in the metaphorical sense, we are all involuntary playgoers at a continuous performance of the absurd drama of global political life. Thus riveted to the "stage," we require a far better awareness of what could happen, a far-reaching lucidity that can anticipate and prevent a frightful *coup de theatre*. To do this, we must understand, with Artistotle, that the purpose of the play is not to excite us with the misfortunes of fellow creatures, but to awaken within us fear for ourselves.

To a certain extent, the no-holds-barred orientation to violence of terrorists stems from pragmatic motives. Faced with a struggle that is typically cast as a zero-sum game, the terrorist suspends those norms of law that customarily mitigate the excesses of armed conflict, and embraces the imperative of a "war of annihilation." Because coexistence and compromise are judged impossible, all efforts are bent toward violence. In the case of Al Fatah, the apocalyptic "battle of vengeance" is expected to galvanize the masses to "feel their active personality and restore their self-confidence."[32]

The no-holds-barred orientation to violence of many modern terrorist groups also stems from the romanticization of brutality that is a dominant motif of terrorist thinking. Even when it is doubtful that excessive and arbitrary force will be productive of their desired goals, terrorists are sometimes moved by Fanon's statement, from *The Wretched of the Earth:* "Violence is a purifying force. It frees the native from his inferiority complex and from despair and inaction. It makes him fearless and restores his self-respect."

This idea, that violence serves not only to injure the opposition but also to transform the revolutionary struggle, lies at the heart of the doctrine of Al Fatah. Any reading of Fatah pamphlets—for example, "The Revolution and Violence, the Road to Victory"—will reveal such thinking. Violence, the reader is told, liberates not only through liquidation of the enemy, but also through its therapeutic and purifying effect on the revolutionary. Violence, stated a Fatah memorandum to Arab journalists, "is a healing medicine for all our people's diseases."[33]

Another basis of the no-holds-barred orientation to violence that is present in modern terrorism lies in the position, articulated by many terrorist groups, that the overwhelming righteousness of their objectives justifies any means whatsoever. Here, of course, terrorists are engaged in the well-known argument "the ends justify the means." The contemporary roots of this argument may be found in Mikhail Bakhunin's elucidation of banditry in nineteenth-century Russia:

> The nature of Russian banditry is cruel and ruthless; yet no less cruel and ruthless is that governmental might which has brought this kind of bandit into being by its wanton acts. Governmental cruelty has engendered the cruelty of the people and made it into something necessary and natural. But between these two cruelties, there still remains a vast difference; the first strives for the complete annihilation of the people, the other endeavors to set them free.[34]

As long as terrorist groups assume such a stance on violent excesses, they are susceptible to what Hannah Arendt has called the "banality of evil" problem. This is the problem in which individuals engage in evil without experiencing it as evil. In certain instances, this problem has even occasioned terrorists to displace responsibility for their own violent acts upon their victims.

Many of today's terrorists are able to avoid individual responsibility for their acts by displacing this responsibility upon the terrorist group itself. By transforming persons into members of the group—into servants of a "higher cause"—feelings of individual responsibility have been submerged by the "psychology of the cell." The effects of this psychology may increase the likelihood of nuclear terrorism.

Terrorist Insensitivity to Orthodox Deterrence

In Act 2 of his play *Henry IV*, Luigi Pirandello reminded us that not all of the players in life's game always abide by the rules, and that calculations that rest upon the foundations of logic crumble before madness: "Do you know what it means to find yourselves face to face with a madman—with one who shakes the foundations of all you have built up in yourselves, your logic, the logic of all your constructions? Madmen, lucky folk, construct without logic, or rather with a logic that flies like a feather."

Understood in terms of the problem of nuclear terrorism, Pirandello's wisdom suggests the limitations of conventional deterrence "logic" as an effective preventive strategy. Although it would certainly be unreasonable to suggest that all terrorists are mad and irrational, it would not be unreasonable to suggest that terrorist groups often operate under a special meaning of rationality. Indeed, as we have seen recently, terrorist operatives are sometimes even willing to die for the cause. This renders them insensitive to the kinds of retaliatory threats that are the traditional mainstay of order between states.

What are the implications of this particular behavioral characteristic of terrorist actors for the threat of nuclear terrorism? Clearly, the most important implication is that terrorists calculating the prospective costs and benefits of nuclear insurgency might ignore the fear of retaliatory destruction. This means that traditional threats of deterrence might have little or no bearing on the terrorist decision concerning use of nuclear force.

A willingness to die for the cause also creates martyrs, which may be helpful to the terrorist purpose. This idea has been best understood by the theoretician Abraham Guillen:

> In a revolutionary war a guerrilla action that needs explaining to the people is politically useless: it should be meaningful and convincing by itself. To kill an ordinary soldier in reprisal for the assassination of a guerrilla is to descend to the same political level as a reactionary army. Far better to create a martyr and thereby attract mass sympathy than to lose or neutralize popular support by senseless killings without an evident political goal.[35]

Although far less instrumental in his understanding of martyrdom in the context of insurgency, Herbert Marcuse also recognized the martyr's contribution:

> Martyrs have rarely helped a political cause, and "revolutionary suicide" remains suicide. And yet, it would be self-righteous indifference to say that the revolutionary ought to live rather than die for the revolution— an insult to the Communards of all times. When the establishment proclaims its professional killers as heroes, and its rebelling victims as criminals, it is hard to save the idea of heroism for the other side. The desperate act, doomed to failure, may for a brief moment tear the veil of justice and expose the faces of brutal suppression; it may arouse the conscience of the neutrals; it may reveal hidden cruelties and lies. Only he who commits the desperate act can judge whether the price he is bound to pay is too high.[36]

Perhaps the most frightening implication of self-sacrificing behavior on the part of terrorists is the idea that similar behavior might be needed for successful counterterrorism. Writing from an ideological point of view fundamentally different from those of Guillen and Marcuse, but in much the same analytic vein, Gerald Priestland offered the following hard observation:

> What the free world has to realize is that, if it wants to remain free, it will, besides maintaining police vigilance, have to accept civilian casualties.

Sooner or later someone will have to give the order to assault a hijacked plane, hostages or no hostages—refuse to release convicted terrorists, whatever the blackmail—turn down demands for aviation fuel, whether or not the plane is blown up in retaliation. If innocent hostages are killed— well, there can never by any adequate solace in any kind of bereavement. But the free world should honor those victims as martyrs in the cause of freedom, and see that their dependants are taken care of even more generously than those of soldiers who fall in battle. Those are hard words to write; but this is the knot of the problem: if men are ready to die for what is wrong, how can the right triumph unless its supporters are ready to die too?[37]

Even when terrorists do not display self-sacrificing characteristics, their unique stance on the balance of risks that can be taken renders them insensitive to orthodox threats of deterrence. Because their willingness to take risks is usually far greater than that of states, the prevention of nuclear terrorism will have to take this into account. In this connection, it is essential that deterrent measures be correlated with the particular terrorist stance on the balance of risks that can be taken. Instead of the usual threats of physically punishing retaliation, deterrence of nuclear terrorism must be based upon threats to obstruct circumstances that terrorists value even more than personal safety.

These circumstances center upon sectors of public support for terrorist goals and strategies. In this connection, we are reminded of the "hunger artist" in Franz Kafka's novella of the same name. For the hunger artist, a professional faster, sustained starvation was hardly a form of punishment. After all, he had—as is made clear in the story—no real appetite for food. However, once his regular coterie of observers and admirers began to drift away from their daily vigil as an enthusiastic audience, he quickly shriveled and died. His true punishment, and the actual cause of his death, lay not in starvation, but in the withdrawal of people from whose admiring looks and exaltations the hunger artist drew his only meaningful nourishment.

In the manner of Kafka's strange character, certain of today's terrorist groups fear the withdrawal of popular interest and support more acutely than they do threats to their physical lives. It follows that because the terrorist's "appetite" for life may actually be subordinate to the need for popular adulation, the key to successful deterrence of nuclear terrorism may lie less in the threat of physical harm than in the removal of an admiring public. To reduce the probability of terrorist nuclear violence, threats should be considered that recognize the wisdom of Kafka's story.

Interterrorist Cooperation

There exists a significant phenomenon in world politics—systematic cooperation and collaboration between terrorist groups. Terrorists have always formed alignments with sympathetic states, but now they are also cementing patterns of alliance with each other. In earlier years, a number of joint operations took place. Most of these cooperative cadres of multinational operational teams involved the Popular Front for the Liberation of Palestine (PFLP). Consider the following events:

> May 1972. Japanese Red Army (JRA)/PFLP/German collaboration in attacking Lod Airport, Israel.
>
> July 1973. PFLP/JRA/Latin American cooperation in hijacking a Japan Air Lines 747 aircraft in Europe.
>
> January 1974. PFLP/JRA operation against Shell Oil facilities in Singapore.
>
> September 1974. JRA/PFLP/Baader-Meinhof collaboration in assault on the French Embassy, The Hague.
>
> January 1975. PFLP/German/Carlos cooperation in attempted attack against El Al aircraft, Orly Airport, Paris.
>
> December 1975. Carlos/German/Palestinian collaboration in the Vienna assault on the ministerial conference of the Organization of Oil Producing and Exporting Countries (OPEC).
>
> June 1976. PFLP/Latin American/German effort culminating at Entebbe.[38]

What are the implications of such cooperation for nucler destruction by terrorists?

First, interterrorist cooperation vastly increases terrorist opportunities for acquiring nuclear weapons. This is especially true when acquisition takes the form of self-development and design from "raw" fissionable materials, as cooperation expands opportunities for both capital and expertise.

Second, cooperation among terrorist groups is apt to encourage the spread of "private" nuclear weapons around the world, creating a network whereby such weapons can be exchanged and transported across national boundaries.

Third, cooperation between terrorists is likely to spread the "benefits" of advanced training in the use of nuclear weapons and the techniques of nuclear reactor sabotage.

Fourth, terrorist cooperation is likely to provide such reciprocal privileges as forged documents and safe-havens, which are needed for pre- and post-attack operations.

Fifth, because much of the cooperative training of terrorists has been conducted under Palestinian direction in Palestinian camps, such training is likely to enlarge the number of targets attractive to the PLO. To a certain extent, as our list of cooperative efforts among terrorists indicates, this enlargement has already taken place as Japanese Red Army, Latin American, and German groups "repaid" George Habash's PFLP with attacks on Israeli personnel and facilities.[39]

Tolerance and Support of Terrorism

Ironically, although terrorists are engaged in "total war" encounters with much of humanity, the prevailing attitude toward them in many countries is still one of tolerance or open support. Consider two prominent examples. First, in the wake of the July 4, 1976, Israeli commando raid at Entebbe, which freed 105 hostages taken by pro-Palestinian skyjackers, African members of the UN Security Council proposed a resolution to condemn the raid as a "flagrant violation" of Uganda's sovereignty. In view of longstanding international law, such a proposal was unjustified as all states have a responsibility to protect nationals of other countries and a corresponding obligation to protect their own nationals in extremis abroad. Second, in the aftermath of Munich, a number of Arab governments heaped lavish praise upon Black September for the 1972 murder of the Israeli athletes in the Olympic Village.

In international relations, the tolerance and support of terrorism by certain states stems from the belief that terrorist groups often work in their own national interests. Issues of morality are overshadowed by the presumption that terrorists, however inadvertently, are useful surrogates in the ongoing struggle for international power and influence.[40] The predictable end of such narrow-minded notions of this struggle has been presaged during earlier periods of human history in which global society has lost its center of values, by periods of frightful barbarism, and by periods still anticipated in Nietzsche's parable on the "death of God."

In Nietzsche's parable (in *The Gay Science*), a madman runs into a village square shouting, "Where is God?" Answering his own question, the madman proceeds to inform the laughing villagers: "God is dead! God remains dead! . . . and we have killed him! . . . I come too early. . . . This tremendous event is still on its way." The madman's "tremendous event" is nothing less than poet William Butler Yeats's description of *The Second Coming*:

Things fall apart; the centre cannot hold;
Mere anarchy is loosed upon the world,
The blood-dimmed tide is loosed, and everywhere
The ceremony of innocence is drowned.

In our own century, a period of human history whose dominant motif has been defined by Auschwitz and Hiroshima, this "tremendous event" is already well under way. With the development of alignments between states and terrorist groups in a nuclear age, we may now be only moments away from its apocalyptic conclusion.

At the moment, a number of countries—for example, Libya, the Soviet Union, Saudi Arabia, Iran, Iraq, Syria, South Africa, and South Yemen—are committed sponsors of such alignments. Significantly, the United States has also sponsored its own terrorists in Nicaragua (contras) and Angola (Unita). As long as this situation prevails, many terrorist groups will continue to interpret aid from sponsor states as an incentive to violence.

The idea of terrorism as surrogate political warfare is hardly a recent development. Even before the 1960s, when state-supported terrorism became commonplace in the Middle East and North Africa, Italian Fascists supported the Croatian *Ustasha* in the assassination of King Alexander in 1934.[41] Today, the surrogate phenomenon has been widely termed "a new type of war," and has received considerable attention in the scholarly literature. In June 1974, in a Rand Corporation paper, Brian Jenkins pointed out that "although the actual amount of violence caused by international terrorism is small compared with war, it has had a destabilizing effect on international order and could become a surrogate for conventional warfare against a nation."[42] According to Jenkins:

> Terrorists, whatever their origin or cause, have demonstrated the possibilities of . . . "surrogate warfare." Terrorism, though now rejected as a legitimate mode of warfare by most conventional military establishments, could become an accepted form of warfare in the future. Terrorists could be employed to provoke international incidents, create alarm in an adversary's country, compel it to divert valuable resources to protect itself, destroy its morale, and carry out specific acts of sabotage. Governments could employ existing terrorist groups to attack their opponents, or they could create their own terrorists. Terrorism requires only a small investment, certainly far less than what it costs to wage conventional war. It can be debilitating to the enemy.[43]

A similar argument was offered by Russell E. Bigney and others, in their "Exploration of the Nature of Future Warfare":

The costs and destructiveness of modern warfare, including insurgent wars, are becoming prohibitive and may exceed net gains. As a result, many nations are looking for alternative means to achieve political and economic dominance over adversary nations. The relative low cost of sponsored terrorism and the disproportionate influence that a small well-trained terrorist group can exert becomes an attractive alternative to war.[44]

Support of international terrorism is also increased to the extent that terrorists influence the foreign policies of host states. For example, the host states, sometimes in combination with allied countries, may act as advocates of the terrorist groups before the tribunal of the state system itself. Such advocacy further legitimizes terrorists as actors in world politics, extending their arena of acceptance and influence.

Proposals to sever the bonds between states and terrorist groups are often based on the idea that all states have a common interest in combatting terrorism. These proposals rest on the erroneous premise that all states value the secure operation of the international diplomatic system more than any objective that might be obtained via terrorist surrogates. Such a premise has its roots in and is affirmed by a basic principle of international law: The legal systems embodied in the constitutions of particular states are part of the international legal order and are, therefore, an interest that all states must defend against attack.

In support of this principle, most texts and treatises on international law have expressed the opinion that a state is forbidden to allow its territory to be used as a base for aggressive operations against another state with which it is not at war. Legal scholar Hersch Lauterpacht formulated the following rule concerning the scope of state responsibility for preventing and repressing insurgent acts of private persons against foreign states:

> International law imposes upon the State the duty of restraining persons within its territory from engaging in such revolutionary activities against friendly States as amount to organized acts of force in the form of hostile expeditions against the territory of those States. It also obliges the State to repress and discourage activities in which attempts against the life of political opponents are regarded as a proper means of revolutionary action.[45]

Lauterpacht's rule reaffirms the *Resolution on the Rights and Duties of Foreign Powers as regards the Established and Recognized Governments in case of Insurrection* adopted by the Institute of International Law in 1900. (Section 3 of Article 2 prohibits a state from allowing a hostile military expedition against an established and recognized government to be organized within its territory.) However, even in obligating states to actively oppose wrongful insurgency directed against other states, his rule falls short of the prescription offered by the eighteenth-century Swiss scholar Emerich de Vattel. According to Book 2 of Vattel's *The Law of Nations,* states that support such insurgency become the lawful prey of other states:

> If there should be found a restless and unprincipled nation, ever ready to do harm to others, to thwart their purposes, and to stir up civil strife among their citizens, there is no doubt that all others would have the right to unite together to subdue such a nation, to discipline it, and even to disable it from doing further harm.

3

Nuclear Terrorism:
Forms and Effects

Nietzsche, in the long critique of faith in his *Antichrist,* wrote, " 'Faith' means not *wanting* to know what is true." Understood in terms of humankind's continuing obliviousness to its own self-destruct tendencies, Nietzsche's point suggests not only cowardice, but also a long-prophesied *Gotterdammerung.* Unless we begin to experience some widespread shocks of recognition about our current nuclear collision course, there is little hope that humankind can escape its last paroxysm.

Spasmodic instances of awareness are not enough. If we are to prevent nuclear catastrophe in world politics, we must begin immediately to hone our anticipatory imagination of what it could entail. The wreckage of moral, spiritual, and physical well-being that would descend in the wake of nuclear terrorism (wreckage that, we shall see, could include nuclear war) must be made more visible if it is to be avoided.

The ground is slowly dissolving under our feet, but we are either unaware of the situation or pretend not to notice. Our pretenses, everyone's pretenses, that irretrievable nuclear disaster cannot happen represent a fatal flight from reality. Our only hope for survival lies in facing the awesome possibilities squarely, and in transforming our primal terrors into constructive strategies of prevention.

Humankind's tendency to flee from a seemingly intolerable reality is communicated brilliantly in Doris Lessing's novel *The Memoirs of a Survivor.* Amidst a dark vision of the not-so-distant future, when humanity gropes for security in a rapidly disintegrating world, the narrator captures our species' peculiar penchant for collective self-delusion:

> For instance, on the newscasts and in the papers they would pursue for days the story of a single kidnapped child, taken from its pram perhaps by some poor unhappy woman. The police would be combing the suburbs and the countryside in hundreds, looking for the child, and for the woman, to punish her. But the next news flash would be about the mass deaths

of hundreds, thousands, or even millions of people. We still believed, wanted to believe, that the first—the concern about the single child, the need to punish the individual criminal, even if it took days and weeks and hundreds of our hard-worked police force to do it—was what really represented us; the second, about the catastrophe, was, as such items of news had always been for people not actually in the threatened area, an unfortunate and minor—or at least not crucial—accident, which interrupted the even flow, the development, of civilization.

There are fissures in the columns of false hopes that sustain our unsteady civilization. These fissures must be enlarged, and the entire edifice of empty expectations destroyed, if a more enduring structure of global society is to be erected. Humankind must learn to spark and nurture deep intimations of a postcatastrophe future as an essential step toward averting such a future. To accomplish this, we must look unflinchingly at the full, unvarnished consequences of nuclear terrorism.

This chapter portrays a landscape of dread. But it must not make us dispirited! Quite the contrary. It must supply us with the motive and the momentum to reorder our hierarchy of concerns.

The kind of play acting described in Lessing's novel can no longer be tolerated in a world teetering at the abyss. The smell of death saturates the air. If it is ignored, we will succumb, not to its repellent olfactory stimuli, but to the blasted orgy of collapse that it forewarns. If it is heeded, as a final presentiment of our species' convulsive rendezvous with extinction, its bitter scent can transform latent potentialities into prodigious efforts at renewal.

In the unsentimental theater of modern world politics, the time is at hand for a new kind of dramaturgy, a "new naturalism" that touches profoundly the deepest rhythms of human imagination. At the same time, we must resurrect the traditional function of theater to evoke pity and terror. The world is pregnant with apocalyptic possibilities. These possibilities must be acknowledged forthrightly, with ruthless frankness, and without sentimentality or shamefaced absentmindedness.

Nuclear Explosives

The low-technology nuclear explosives that might be manufactured by terrorists could range anywhere from a few hundred tons to several kilotons in yield. The destructive potential of such explosives would depend on such variables as type of construction, population density, prevailing wind direction, weather patterns, and the characteristic features of the target area. Such potential would be manifested in terms of three primary effects: *blast* (measured in pounds per square inch of overpressure); *heat* (measured in calories/cm²); and *radiation* (measured in Radiation Effective Man—REM—a combined measure that includes the Radiation Absorbed Dose—RAD—and the Radiation Biological Effectiveness—RBE—or the varying biological effectiveness of different types of radiation).

Relatively crude nuclear explosives with yields equivalent to about 1,000 tons of high explosive would be far easier to fabricate than explosives with yields equivalent to about 10 kilotons of high explosive.[1] Nonetheless, explosives with a yield of only one-tenth of a kiloton would pose significant destructive effects. A nuclear explosive in this limited range could annihilate the Capitol during the State of the Union Address or knock down the World Trade Center towers in New York City. An even smaller yield of 10 tons of TNT could kill everyone attending the Super Bowl.[2]

In assessing the destructiveness of nuclear explosions, it is important to remember that such explosions are typically more damaging than chemical explosions of equivalent yields. This is the case because nuclear explosions produce energy in the form of penetrating radiations (gamma rays and neutrons) as well as in blast wave and heat. Moreover, a nuclear explosion on the ground—the kind of nuclear explosion most likely to be used by terrorists—produces *more* local fallout than a comparable explosion in the air.[3]

It is conceivable, of course, that terrorists might seek to steal an assembled nuclear weapon. At the moment, it is doubtful that all nuclear-weapons states provide for comprehensive protection of deployed and stored nuclear weapons. To reduce the risk of theft of assembled nuclear weapons by terrorists, these states will need to improve protective devices (especially Permissive Action Link, or PAL, systems with "limited try" and "command disable" features); enhance command, control, and communications systems for deployment and use of nuclear weapons; and strengthen capabilities to recover stolen weapons.[4] Without such measures, the kinds of nuclear explosions that could be detonated by terrorists could include many forms of tactical nuclear weapons (for example, forward land-based nuclear weapons in NATO, naval tactical nuclear weapons, and tactical nuclear weapons stored in the United States).

Still another problem involves the possible marriage of nuclear explosives manufactured by terrorists with short-range ballistic missiles. Should terrorists become capable of placing such self-developed explosives on stolen missiles, their capacity for "deep penetration" nuclear destruction and blackmail would be very high. Although the technology associated with such nuclear weapons would necessarily be extremely crude, access to both components is already within reach. As indicated in a recent study by the Congressional Research Service, the proliferation of ballistic missiles in the Third World has begun, and the ability to indigenously produce such systems is rapidly spreading.[5]

Radiological Weapons

Radiological weapons are not as widely understood as nuclear explosives, but they are equally ominous in their effects. Placed in the hands of terrorists, such weapons could pose a lethal hazard for human beings anywhere in the world. Even a world already dominated by every variety of numbing could not fail to recoil from such a prospect.

Radiological weapons are devices designed to disperse radioactive materials that have been produced a substantial time before their dispersal. The targets against which terrorists might choose to use radiological weapons include concentrations of people inside buildings, concentrations of people on urban streets or at sports events, urban areas with a high population density as a whole, and agricultural areas.[6] The form such weapons might take include plutonium dispersal devices (only 3.5 ounces of plutonium could prove lethal to everyone within a large office building or factory) or devices designed to disperse other radioactive materials. In principle, the dispersal of spent nuclear reactor fuel and the fission products separated from reactor fuels would create grave hazards in a populated area, but the handling of such materials would be very dangerous to terrorists themselves. It is more likely, therefore, that would-be users of radiological weapons would favor plutonium over radioactive fission products.[7]

The threat of nuclear terrorism involving radiological weapons is potentially more serious than the threat involving nuclear explosives. This is because it would be easier for terrorists to achieve nuclear capability with radiological weapons. Such weapons, therefore, could also be the subject of a more plausible hoax than nuclear explosives.

Nuclear Reactor Sabotage

In the aftermath of the Chernobyl disaster, even the average layperson has become familiar with the meaning of "reactor-core meltdown." Such an event, in which a reactor deprived of its temperature-controlling coolant melts in its own heat and produces lethal clouds of radioactive gases, could be the objective of future terrorism. Significantly, as we shall see, incidents involving violence or threats of violence at nuclear facilities at home and abroad are already a matter of record.

In comparison with a low-yield nuclear explosion, a reactor-core meltdown and breach of containment would release a small amount of radiation.[8] However, the consequences of such an event would still involve leakage of an immense amount of gaseous radioactive material that could expose neighboring populations to immediate death, cancer, or genetic defects. To better understand the nature of the threat, we must first try to understand the fundamentals of nuclear reactors.

Essentially, these reactors may be characterized as giant teakettles that turn water into steam. The steam is piped to large turbines that turn generators. When a typical teakettle is operating at full power, the radioactivity in its fuel core can reach 17 billion curies, enough—in principle—to kill everyone on the planet. Within the uranium fuel rods in the core, the fission reaction can unleash energy to drive the temperature above 4,000 degrees Farenheit—a temperature hot enough to melt through all protective barriers.[9]

In assessing the dangers of nuclear power reactors, the Rasmussen Report expected an extremely serious accident (which would closely resemble sabotage in its effects) to produce 3,300 prompt fatalities, 45,000 instances of early illness, 240,000 thyroid nodules over a 30-year period, and 30,000 genetic defects over 150 years. Additionally, the economic loss that would result from contamination over an area of 3,200 square miles was estimated at $14 billion.[10]

On July 1, 1977, the U.S. Nuclear Regulatory Commission organized the Risk Assessment Review Group. The group's purpose was to "clarify the achievements and limitations of the Rasmussen Report, WASH-1400, to study the state of such risk assessment methodology, and to recommend whether and how such methodology can be used in the licensing and regulation of reactors."[11] The group concluded that WASH-1400 had been conservative in certain respects, particularly as regards the overall probability of core melt.

Although finding WASH-1400 to be "a conscientious and honest effort" to assess nuclear reactor safety,[12] the Risk Assessment Review Group identified nagging doubts about that effort's probability calculations. Among these doubts, the following was highlighted in the group's summary:

. . . inability to quantify human adaptability during the course of an accident, and a pervasive regulatory influence in the choice of uncertain parameters, while among the latter are nagging issues about completeness, and an inadequate treatment of common cause failure. We are unable to define whether the overall probability of a core melt given in WASH-1400 is high or low, but we are certain that the error bands are understated. We cannot say by how much. Reasons for this include an inadequate data base, a poor statistical treatment, an inconsistent propagation of uncertainties throughout the calculation, etc.[13]

In the group's statement of findings, WASH-1400 is characterized, despite its stated shortcomings, as "the most complete single picture of accident probabilities associated with nuclear reactors." At the same time, the following points were also made:

- The dispersion model for radioactive material developed in WASH-1400 for reactor sites as a class cannot be applied to individual sites without significant refinement and sensitivity tests.
- The biological effects models should be updated and improved in the light of new information.
- After having studied the peer comments about some important classes of initiating events, we are unconvinced of the correctness of the WASH-1400 conclusion that they contribute negligibly to the overall risk. Examples include fires, earthquakes, and human accident initiation.
- The statistical analysis in WASH-1400 leaves much to be desired. It suffers from a spectrum of problems, ranging from lack of data on which to base input distributions to the invention and use of wrong statistical methods. Even when the analysis is done correctly, it is often presented in so murky a way as to be very hard to decipher.
- For a report of this magnitude, confidence in the correctness· of the results can only come from a systematic and deep peer review process. The peer review process of WASH-1400 was defective in many ways and the review was inadequate.
- Lack of scrutability is a major failing of the report, impairing both its usefulness and the quality of possible peer review.
- The Executive Summary to WASH-1400, which is by far the most widely read part of the report among the public and policy makers, does not adequately indicate the full extent of the consequences of reactor accidents; and does not sufficiently emphasize the uncertainties involved in the calculation of their probability. It has therefore lent itself to misuse in the discussion of reactor risk.
- WASH-1400 was directed to make a "realistic" estimate of risk. In the regulatory process, the usual conservatisms must be incorporated. There have been instances in which WASH-1400 has been misused as a vehicle to judge the acceptability of reactor risks. In other cases, it may have been used prematurely as an estimate of the absolute risk of reactor accidents without full realization of the wide band of uncertainties involved. Such use should be discouraged.[14]

According to data made available to the International Task Force on Prevention of Nuclear Terrorism, some 155 bombings, other attacks, and violent demonstrations have taken place at sites of civil nuclear installations in Europe and the United States over the past twenty years. Most of these incidents have taken place near power reactors. None has caused a serious accident. Yet, "a reactor accident brought about by terrorists, even one releasing significant amounts of radioactivity, is by no means implausible and is technically feasible."[15]

Significantly, despite the NRC mandate to protect the U.S. public from certain risks associated with nuclear terrorism, some critics charge that too little has been done to reduce these risks. According to Daniel Hirsch and Stephanie Murphy's report to the Safeguards and Security Subcommittee, Advisory Committe on Reactor Safeguards:

> Despite a radical increase in the incidence and nature of terrorist and other attacks worldwide, the required level of protection at power reactors has remained unchanged for nearly a decade, and, despite no change in the regulations, NRC Staff has undertaken unilateral actions which would have the effect of reducing substantially the level of protection at non-power reactors. This combination of negative action and inaction has created a dangerous situation, with reactors insufficiently protected against the kinds of real threats that exist in world today.[16]

Nuclear reactors, of course, may make tempting targets for terrorist attack in other countries as well. Approximately 370 nuclear power plants are now operating in twenty-seven countries, with a like number under construction. By the end of this century, perhaps forty countries will be producing electricity with large, commercial nuclear reactors. Even if each of these facilities is constructed with scrupulous attention to safety from terrorist attack, their vulnerability to willful destruction through disruption of coolant mechanisms will be high.[17] And reactor vulnerability is apt to increase with the spread of precision-guided munitions throughout national arsenals.[18]

From the standpoint of radiation discharged, the consequences of a successful conventional attack upon nuclear reactors could equal those of the worst accidental meltdown. According to Bennett Ramberg, this form of nuclear terrorism could result in moderate to major releases of radioactivity into the environment:

> A moderate release from a reactor the size of Three Mile Island—880 megawatts of electricity—that has been operating for more than three months could contaminate 500 square miles; a major release might affect 2000–5000 square miles and require occupation restrictions for perhaps decades, as the effectiveness of decontamination is very uncertain. Since nations often cluster several reactors, the problems would be compounded if the contents of more than one were discharged, as is conceivable in military scenarios. Additional problems would arise through release of the inventories of spent fuel customarily located at reactor sites. Early fatalities are possible, although late cancers and genetic effects would dominate. In densely populated countries deaths could number in the tens of thousands.[19]

Whatever form nuclear terrorism might take—nuclear explosives, radiological weapons, or nuclear reactor sabotage—its effects would be social and political as well as biological and physical. In the aftermath of a nuclear terrorist event, both governments and insurgents would be confronted with mounting pressures to escalate to higher-order uses of force. With terrorists more inclined to think of nuclear weapons as manifestly "thinkable," both governments and terrorists would find themselves giving serious consideration to striking first.

Like Camus' Caligula, who kills because "there's only one way of getting even with the gods . . . to be as cruel as they," a number of terrorist groups could turn to nuclear weaponry as a promising new instrument of vengeance. Faced with such threats, governments would find it necessary to choreograph their own macabre dances of death, meeting savagery with savagery in a quest for security that might reveal only impotence. In the wake of such widespread dislocation, madness would be celebrated by all sides as the liberating core of survival, and sanity would dissolve into insignificance.

It is not a pretty picture. The record of human history reveals not only the most extreme manifestations of deliberate evil, but also the most bizarre and inexplicable attraction to that evil. Living, as we must, with both the memory and the expectation of holocaust, the "pornography of death" that lies latent in the prospect of nuclear terrorism carries not only the dark vision of cosmic disorder, but also the deformation of the human spirit through successive imitations of excessive violence.

Nuclear Terrorism and Nuclear War

Nuclear terrorism could even spark full-scale war between states. Such war could involve the entire spectrum of nuclear-conflict possibilities, ranging from a nuclear attack upon a non-nuclear state to systemwide nuclear war. How might such far-reaching consequences of nuclear terrorism come about? Perhaps the most likely way would involve a terrorist nuclear assault against a state by terrorists hosted in another state. For example, consider the following scenario:

Early in the 1990s, Israel and its Arab-state neighbors finally stand ready to conclude a comprehensive, multilateral peace settlement. With a bilateral treaty between Israel and Egypt already many years old, only the interests of the Palestinians—as defined by the PLO—seem to have been left out. On the eve of the proposed signing of the peace agreement, half a dozen crude nuclear explosives in the one-kiloton range detonate in as many Israeli cities. Public grief in Israel over the many thousands dead and maimed is matched only by the outcry for revenge. In response to the public mood, the government of Israel initiates selected strikes against terrorist strongholds in Lebanon, whereupon Lebanese Shiite forces and Syria retaliate against Israel. Before long, the entire region is ablaze, conflict has escalated to nuclear forms, and all countries in the area have suffered unprecedented destruction.

Of course, such a scenario is fraught with the makings of even wider destruction. How would the United States react to the situation in the Middle East? What would be the Soviet response? It is certainly conceivable that a chain reaction of interstate nuclear conflict could ensue, one that would ultimately involve the superpowers or even every nuclear-weapons state on the planet.

What, exactly, would this mean? Whether the terms of assessment be statistical or human, the consequences of nuclear war require an entirely new paradigm of death. Only such a paradigm would allow us a proper framework for absorbing the vision of near-total obliteration and the outer limits of human destructiveness. Any nuclear war would have effectively permanent and irreversible consequences. Whatever the actual extent of injuries and fatalities, such a war would entomb the spirit of the entire species in a planetary casket strewn with shorn bodies and imbecile imaginations.

This would be as true for a "limited" nuclear war as for an "unlimited" one. Contrary to continuing Pentagon commitments to the idea of selected "counterforce" strikes that would allegedly reduce the chances for escalation and produce fewer civilian casualties, the strategy of limited nuclear war is inherently unreasonable. There is, in fact, no clear picture of what states might hope to gain from counterforce attacks. This understanding is reflected by Soviet military strategy, which is founded on the idea that any nuclear conflict would necessarily be unlimited.

Nuclear War Between the Superpowers

The consequences of a strategic exchange between the United States and the Soviet Union have been the object of widespread attention. One early account of these consequences was offered by Andrei D. Sakharov:

A complete destruction of cities, industry, transport, and systems of education, a poisoning of fields, water, and air by radioactivity, a physical destruction of the larger part of mankind, poverty, barbarism, a return to savagery, and a genetic degeneracy of the survivors under the impact of radiation, a destruction of the material and information basis of civilization—this is a measure of the peril that threatens the world as a result of the estrangement of the world's two superpowers.[20]

Presently, U.S. arsenals contain approximately 12,000 strategic nuclear weapons. Soviet strategic forces number approximately 9,000 weapons.

When the tactical nuclear inventories are counted (mines, artillery, torpedoes, cruise missiles, etc.), the two superpowers have approximately 48,000 nuclear weapons (97 percent of the world's total).[21] An exchange involving any substantial fractions of these forces could promptly destroy more than half of the urban populations in both countries. The subsequent fallout could be expected to kill upwards of 50 percent of the surviving rural inhabitants as well as create worldwide contamination of the atmosphere.[22]

To better understand the effects of fallout, it is useful to recognize that radiation effects have three basic forms: (1) radiation directly from the explosion; (2) immediate radioactive fallout (first twenty-four hours); and (3) long-term fallout (months and years). In areas where radioactive fallout is of particularly high intensity, individuals will be exposed to high doses of radiation regardless of shelter protection. Those who do not become prompt or short-term fatalities and have suffered radiation exposures above 100 REMs will undergo hemotological (blood system) alterations that diminish immunological capabilities. The resultant vulnerability to infection will seriously impair prospects for long-term recovery.[23]

The effects of a nuclear war between the superpowers, however, cannot be understood solely in terms of projected casualties. Rather, these effects must also include quantitative effects (availability of productive capacity, fuel, labor, food, and other resources); qualitative effects (political, social, and psychological damage); and interactive effects (the impact on the relationships between the social and economic factors of production).[24] When these corollary effects are taken into account, it is easy to see that policymakers and public alike have, until recently, understated the aggregate impact of nuclear war.

This point was supported by a 1975 study of the National Research Council, National Academy of Sciences (NAS), entitled *Long-Term Worldwide Effects of Multiple Nuclear Weapons Detonations*. Going beyond the usual litany of crude physical measures of destruction (e.g., number of human fatalities, number of cities destroyed), the report portrayed the long-term, worldwide effects following a hypothetical exchange of 10,000 megatons of explosive power in the northern hemisphere. These effects are cast in terms of atmosphere and climate, natural terrestrial ecosystems, agriculture and animal husbandry, the aquatic environment, and both somatic and genetic changes in human populations.[25]

Although the report recognized that the biosphere and the species *Homo sapiens* would survive the hypothesized nuclear war, it recognized that the very idea of survival in such a context is problematic. Building upon this recognition, a later study prepared for the Joint Committee on Defense Production of the Congress—*Economic and Social Consequences of Nuclear Attacks on the United States*—identified four discrete levels of postattack survival. This new taxonomy permitted a more subtle look at the interactive effects of nuclear war and allowed more precise judgments about the acceptability or unacceptability of nuclear attack damage. According to the study, there are four levels of survival, in decreasing order of damage.

1. *Biological Survival of Individuals.* Individuals or groups of individuals survive but not necessarily within the organized political, social, and economic structure of a modern society.
2. *Regional Survival of Political Structures.* Some subnational political units survive as viable entities, but without a functioning central government.
3. *Survival of a Central Government.* Some forms of viable, central control over all preattack national territory survives, but the effectiveness of this control may vary over an extremely wide range, depending on the specific nature and pattern of the attack(s).
4. *Survival Intact of Basic Societal Structure.* Damage to the nation is characterized as relatively limited socially, politically, and economically; nevertheless, the attack is militarily destructive. This is the concept of survival envisioned in the notion of limited or controlled nuclear war. However, it should be noted that the idea that effective strategic military attacks can be benign in their impacts on society is in dispute. It is used here as a criterion without any implicit acceptance that it can be achieved.[26]

There are, however, levels of strategic exchange at which even the first listed category of survival might not be relevant. At such levels, the species itself—let alone the organized political, social, and economic structures—would disappear. The plausibility of such levels is underscored by the fact that the magnitude of exchange postulated in the NAS report is really quite low. Were the superpowers to exchange more megatons of nuclear explosives than the 10,000 megatons assumed by the report, worldwide climatological changes would imperil the physical existence of *Homo sapiens.*

One fact is clear. A nuclear war between the superpowers must be considered as we would any other incurable disease: The only hope lies in prevention. Even if an evacuation could be accomplished in time, there is no reason to believe that host areas would be free of lethal radioactivity. Indeed, within weeks after an exchange involving only 5,000 megatons between the superpowers, soot, smoke, and dust from nuclear fires and ground bursts would reduce the amount of sunlight at ground level to a few percent of what is normal. According to comments by astronomer Carl Sagan at a conference on "The World

After Nuclear War" held on October 31, 1983, "An unbroken gloom would persist for weeks over the Northern Hemisphere."[27]

But this would be only the beginning. For the succeeding months, the light filtering through this pall would be unable to sustain photosynthesis. As a result, a devastating impairment of the process whereby plants convert sunlight to food would take place—an impairment that would cascade through all food chains and produce long-term famine.

The lack of sunlight could also produce a harsh "nuclear winter" with temperatures dropping by as much as 25 degrees centigrade in inland areas. Many regions could be subject to continuous snowfall, even in the summer. In addition to killing all crops in the Northern Hemisphere, a nuclear war between the superpowers would freeze surface waters in the interior of continents, causing a great many animals to die of thirst.[28]

These effects, of course, would accompany an exchange that could immediately kill 1.1 billion people and severely injure the same number. Moreover, because radioactive debris in huge amounts—an estimated 225 million tons in a few days, according to Sagan—would be carried throughout the atmosphere, exposure to radioactive fallout would likely be not only nationwide but worldwide. In addition, urban fires set off by the nuclear blasts would generate large amounts of deadly toxins by vaporizing the huge stockpiles of stored synthetic chemicals.

The most devastating effects would be long-term. Contrary to conclusions supported by our leaders, nuclear war would have a major effect on climate lasting for several years. High-yield nuclear explosions would inject nitrogen oxides into the stratosphere, resulting in large reductions of the ozone layer. Because this layer screens the earth from excessive amounts of ultraviolet (UV) radiation, its reduction could have a marked impact on microorganisms in the soil and on aquatic life.

Worldwide Nuclear War

If nuclear terrorism should lead to worldwide nuclear war, the results would represent humankind's last and most complete calamity, defying not only our imaginations of disaster, but our customary measurements as well. As the culmination of what Camus once described as "years of absolutely insane history," worldwide nuclear war would represent the final eradication of the very boundaries of annihilation.

In technical terms, the consequences of systemwide nuclear war would include atmospheric effects, effect on natural terrestrial ecosystems, effects on managed terrestrial ecosystems, and effects on the aquatic environment.

Atmospheric effects would be highlighted by greatly reduced ozone concentrations producing increased ultraviolet radiation and a drop in average temperature. Even the possibility of irreversible climatic shifts cannot be ruled out.[29]

Natural Terrestrial Ecosystems would be affected by systemwide nuclear war through three principal stress factors: ionizing radiation; uv-B radiation; and climatic change. The cumulative effects of these three factors would render the entire planet a "hot spot," where even vast forests would show physiological and genetic damage.[30]

Managed Terrestrial Ecosystems would be affected by systemwide nuclear war by radionuclide contamination of foods, chromosome breakage and gene mutations in crops, and yield-reducing sterility in seed crops. The cumulative effect of these changes would be the disappearance of the technology base for agriculture. Even if there were any significant number of human survivors, a return to normal world food production would be unimaginable.[31]

Aquatic effects of a systemwide nuclear war would stem from ionizing radiation from radionuclides in marine waters and freshwaters; solar uv radiation; and changes in water temperatures associated with climate. Irreversible injuries to sensitive aquatic species could be anticipated during the years of large transient increase in uv-B isolation. And the range of geographic distribution of sensitive populations of aquatic organisms could be reduced.[32]

Other Forms of Nuclear War

Nuclear war between the superpowers and worldwide nuclear war are only two forms of strategic conflict that might be sparked by nuclear terrorism. Other forms include a nuclear attack upon a non-nuclear state; a two-country strategic exchange involving secondary nuclear powers; nuclear exchanges between several secondary nuclear powers; nuclear exchanges between secondary nuclear powers and one of the superpowers; nuclear exchanges between secondary nuclear powers and both of the superpowers; and nuclear exchanges between secondary nuclear powers plus one of the superpowers on the one side and other secondary nuclear powers on the opposing side. Although there is apt to be a significant difference in consequences between these forms of nuclear war, some important regularities do emerge.

For example, whatever the kinds of weapons used, their yields, their altitudes of detonation, and the prevailing weather patterns, wide swaths of destruction would be produced by thermal radiation, nuclear radiation, and blast. Individuals would suffer flash and flame burns. Retinal burns could occur in the eyes of persons at distances of several hundred miles from the explosion. People would be crushed by collapsing buildings and torn by flying glass. Others would fall victim to firestorms and fallout injuries. The latter injuries would include whole-body radiation injury, superficial radiation burns, and injuries produced by the deposition of radioactive substances within the body.[33]

Virtually all medical facilities and personnel would become inoperative. Those that might still exist would be taxed beyond endurance. Faced with victims suffering from multiple injuries—combinations of burn, blast, and radiation injuries—surviving physicians would inevitably resort to triage practice—a system for allocating medical resources in disaster conditions whereby the least injured and most injured receive no medical treatment.[34]

Complicating the critical inadequacy of postwar medical care would be unusable water supplies, disappearance of housing and shelter, and the complete breakdown of transportation and communication systems. Emergency police and fire services would be decimated, all systems of electrical power operation would cease functioning, and severe trauma would occasion widespread disorientation for which there would be no available therapy.

Normal society would be a thing of the past: The pestilence of wanton murder and banditry would exacerbate the presence of plague and epidemics. With the passage of time, many of the survivors would fall victim to degenerative diseases and various forms of cancer. And they might also expect premature death, impaired vision, and an increased probability of sterility.

Aristotle, in his *Poetics,* maintained that the playgoer, upon witnessing a great tragedy, undergoes a purgation of soul, a catharsis, out of pity and terror for the characters' and his own lot. In the years ahead, we are all likely to become involuntary playgoers at a performance in the absurd theater of contemporary international life. This performance could take place anywhere in the world, and would involve the enactment of nuclear terrorism in any of its myriad forms. Through the miracle of today's instantaneous communications technology, virtually all of the inhabitants of this endangered planet would be riveted to the stage. It is doubtful, however, that many of us would experience the kind of catharsis described by Aristotle. Rather, our sentiments, for the most part, would display little or no concern for the fate of the victims. The truest catharsis, ironically enough, would almost certainly be felt by the terrorists, whose very purpose in performing would be the need for spectacular self-assertion. Imbued with devotion to the "creativity" of violence, their drama would act out the ritualistic urgings of destructive passion. At the final curtain, these players would celebrate their liberation of irrepressible violence.

But the play doesn't have to end this way. In fact, it need not be performed at all. Bertolt Brecht, whose critical writing on the theater has had a profound effect on twentieth-century drama, once remarked that the actor performs according to the wishes of the audience. Indeed, said Brecht, "he is entirely dependent on the audience, blindly subject to it."[35] Understood in terms of the prospect of nuclear terrorism, Brecht's wisdom suggests a compelling need for more general awareness of what could happen, for a far-reaching lucidity to uncover the terrible possibilities and produce alternate cues.

PART TWO

Preventing Nuclear Terrorism

Introduction

The utopianizing of Robert Owen, the nineteenth-century Welsh reformer, inspired the following lines of the poem "New Harmony" by Adrien Stoutenberg:

> All that was needed was a plan
> to build a terrestrial paradise
> where men, not angels, could convene
> around the circular throne of hope.

We, too, need such a "plan," not for a "terrestrial paradise," but for avoiding the maelstrom of unplumbed depths threatened by nuclear terrorism. Without such a plan to snatch us from the hazardous flux of an absurd world politics, hope could give way to the silent completeness of a desolated planet.

Of course, we may, as a species, fall victim to such an apocalyptic end anyway. A number of present-day cosmologists believe that the universe exhibits neither point nor purpose, but is merely an infinitely repeating series of accidental bounces. In contrast to the biblical version of creation, this model describes a "closed" universe, one that explodes, expands, falls back on itself, and explodes again, eternally. It means, in short, that the universe undergoes infinite reconstitution, and that every event undergoes eternal recurrence. If this model were correct, then there would really be no reason to search for a plan. The pointlessness of the closed universe would ensure the pointlessness of reformist hopes.

But we really don't know if the universe is open or closed, and it would surely be prudent—in the absence of a persuasive master theory— to assume the singularity of an explosive genesis and of subsequent human events. To assume otherwise would be to make certain that what might not have been fated would nevertheless take place through inaction. In this regard, we would do well to heed the words of the Chorus in Swiss dramatist Max Frisch's play, *The Firebugs:*

> Just because it happened,
> Don't put the blame on God,

Nor on our human nature,
Nor on our fruitful earth,
Nor on our radiant sun. . . .
Just because it happened,
Must you call the damned thing Fate?

We must act! It would be folly to accept the ebbing of planetary life with autumnal resignation. We *do* need a plan. And we must heighten the consciousness of general publics throughout the world to this need.

This plan must be more than the usual commitment to a mélange of laws, treaties, and safeguards. Of course, such modalities of counterterrorist strategy are essential to the avoidance of nuclear catastrophe, and they will be carefully developed in the following three chapters. But they are not enough. What is also needed, and what must inform the entire configuration of technical/legal/political/military remedies, is an entirely new orientation to international political life. This orientation must replace the existing separation of conflictual nations from global community with a new understanding of the benefits of interrelatedness.

The states in world politics must begin to fashion their foreign policies on a new set of premises, one that defines national interest in terms of what is best for the world system as a whole. By supplanting competitive self-seeking with cooperative self-seeking, and by renouncing the "everyone for himself" principle in world affairs, states can begin to move away from the social-Darwinian ethic that would otherwise assure our oblivion. By building upon the understanding that it is in each state's best interests to develop foreign policy from a systemic vantage point, and by defining national interests in terms of strategies that secure and sustain the entire system of states, our national leaders can begin to match the awesome agenda of world order reform with effective strategies of response. With such a starting point, the prevention of global nuclear catastrophe could draw its animating vision from the wisdom of Pierre Teilhard de Chardin: "The egocentric ideal of a future reserved for those who have managed to attain egoistically the extremity of 'everyone for himself' is false and against nature. No element could move and grow except with and by all the others with itself" (*The Phenomenon of Man*).

The false communion of nation-states is inwardly rotten, time-dishonored, close to collapsing. A communion based on fear and dread, its mighty efforts at producing increasingly destructive weapons have occasioned a deep desolation of the human spirit. The world has conquered technology only to lose its soul.

"The world, as it is now," Herman Hesse wrote in *Demian*, about the first quarter of the present century, "wants to die, wants to perish—

and it will." No doubt, were he alive today, Hesse would see no need to change that observation. Indeed, as an anticipatory vision of what lies ahead, his observation is more exquisitely attuned to the present moment than to its intended time. Recognizing this fact, the following chapters are conceived with a view to altering this vision, to rendering it inaccurate. To accomplish this, international *angst* must give way to community, and humanity's store of international ideals must yield a gentle and new harmony.

4

Hardening the Target: Physical Security and Nonproliferation

In Franz Kafka's terrifying novella *The Metamorphosis* Gregor Samsa—the central figure—awakes one morning to find himself transformed into a gigantic insect. Confronted by the awful realization that their son is vermin who must be shut out from the human circle, Gregor's parents evaluate different strategies for dealing with the strange creature. Frau Samsa, diagnosing her son's plight as illness, sends for the doctor. But Herr Samsa, seeing only hostility and disobedience in Gregor's condition, sends for the locksmith. Gregor himself is heartened by both calls for help, and remarks that he cannot really distinguish between the role of the doctor and that of the locksmith.

This story is pertinent to our concern with preventing nuclear terrorism because we, too, must decide between the "doctor" and the "locksmith," between changing the condition of the terrorist pathology or placing new locks on the terrorist potential for violence. To date, the locksmith has been far more popular than the doctor. Defining the threat in physical security terms, governments have consistently focused their attention and resources on the search for a mechanical/technological fix. As a result, the prevention of nuclear terrorism continues to be characterized by an all-consuming preoccupation with guards, firearms, fences, and space-age protection devices.

Of course, if the locksmith is to be truly helpful in preventing nuclear terrorism, physical security measures will have to be implemented internationally. In this connection, special efforts must be made to ensure the success of the nonproliferation regime and to encourage broad international acceptance of International Atomic Energy Agency security standards. Until access to nuclear fuel and assembled nuclear weapons is controlled on a worldwide basis, even the best unilateral measures will be inadequate.

Preventing Nuclear Terrorism
Through Improved Physical Security

To prevent nuclear terrorism, physical barriers must be established that block access to strategic special nuclear materials, nuclear reactors, and nuclear weapons. With this in mind, a growing counter-nuclear-terrorism technology is being developed. This technology, which is designed to raise the prospective costs of "going nuclear," includes better guard forces, fences, sensors, closed-circuit televisions, metal detectors, tags for explosives, and secure communications links.

In the United States, as we have already seen, the protection of nuclear materials is the responsibility of the Department of Energy and the Nuclear Regulatory Commission. To ensure a high level of protection for strategic special nuclear materials and nuclear reactors, the Nuclear Regulatory Commission has for several years been engaged in additional safeguards projects. Although such efforts at sound physical security are far from perfect, they do define some of the kinds of strategies that need to be replicated on a global basis.

With references to the protection of assembled nuclear weapons, principal responsibility in the United States rests with the Department of Defense. From the standpoint of effective worldwide standards for nuclear weapons, it appears that the most promising course would involve widespread imitation and replication of the best of those measures and procedures developed by the U.S. Defense Department. These measures and procedures, which are continually being upgraded and scrutinized, include a Permissive Action Link (PAL) program, which consists of "a code system and a family of devices integral or attached to nuclear weapons that have been developed to reduce the probability of an unauthorized nuclear detonation"; a Personnel Reliability Program (PRP), which consists of a continual screening and evaluation of nuclear-duty personnel to assure reliability; a series of storage area classifications that delineate viable zones of protection; an Intrusion Detection Alarm (IDA) system; security forces capable of withstanding and repelling seizure efforts by terrorists; two-person concept control during any operation that may afford access to nuclear weapons, whereby "a minimum of two (2) authorized personnel, each capable of detecting incorrect or unauthorized procedures with respect to the task to be performed and familiar with applicable safety and security requirements, shall be present"; counterintelligence and investigative services to actively seek information concerning threats to nuclear weapons; and carefully worked out logistic movement procedures, to ensure nuclear-weapons security in transit.[1]

Preventing Nuclear Terrorism Through Nonproliferation

The present nonproliferation regime is based upon a series of multilateral agreements, statutes, and safeguards. The principal elements of this series are the U.S. Atomic Energy Act of 1954; the Statute of the International Atomic Energy Agency, which came into force in 1957; the Nuclear Test Ban Treaty, which entered into force on October 10, 1963; the Outer Space Treaty, which entered into force on October 10, 1967; the Treaty Prohibiting Nuclear Weapons in Latin America, which entered into force on April 22, 1968; and the Seabeds Arms Control Treaty, which entered into force on May 18, 1972.

The single most important element of the nonproliferation regime, however, is the Treaty on the Non-Proliferation of Nuclear Weapons (NPT), which entered into force on March 5, 1970. As Article 6 of this treaty calls for an end to the nuclear arms race between the superpowers,[2] the current vertical arms control negotiations must also be counted as part of the nonproliferation regime. Before the world's non-nuclear powers can begin to take nonproliferation seriously, the United States and the Soviet Union will have to take prompt steps to bring their own nuclear armaments under control. At the moment there is a great deal of worldwide disenchantment about the fact that the two nuclear superpowers have not yet given meaningful content to that pledge.

In the view of the non-nuclear-weapons states, a "bargain" has been struck between the superpowers and themselves. Unless the Soviet Union and the United States begin to take more ambitious steps toward implementation of the Article 6 pledge, they, too, will move in the direction of nuclear capability. The non-nuclear powers consider this bargain the most prudential path to safety.

From the standpoint of controlling nuclear proliferation and preventing nuclear terrorism, this suggests that the superpowers must restructure their central strategic relationship. Such restructuring must be oriented toward a return to strategies of "minimum deterrence," a comprehensive nuclear test ban; a U.S. renunciation of first use of nuclear weapons; a joint nuclear freeze; and a joint effort toward creating additional nuclear-weapon-free zones.

Minimum Deterrence

First, the United States and the Soviet Union must return to the relative sanity of strategies based upon the ability to inflict overwhelming damage upon the aggressor after absorbing a nuclear first strike.[3] It is widely understood that each side now has far more weaponry than is necessary for minimum deterrence. Because the survival of even the smallest fraction of U.S. or Soviet ICBMs, bombers, and submarines could assure the destruction of the other, we now have multiple levels of overkill. No conceivable breakthrough in military technology can upset either side's minimum deterrence capability. Within the structure of current arms control deliberations, the return to minimum deterrence must involve major commitments to further strategic-weapons reductions, more comprehensive qualitative constraints on new strategic-weapon systems, provisions for improved verification, and, above all else, an end to U.S. efforts to achieve "strategic defense."

The government of the United States has yet to admit to its citizens that they must be utterly defenseless against the effects of nuclear weapons. Reliable ballistic missile defense has never existed, nor will it ever exist. Ironically, the attempt to institute such defenses is extraordinarily provocative, as it will encourage the Soviet Union to accelerate its offensive missile capabilities and even to preempt in the near term. The United States, for its part, lulled into complaisance by the delusion of defense, might abandon remaining plans for arms control or even fulfill Soviet fears by preparing for a U.S. first strike.

Even if strategic defense *were* feasible, it could only degrade the security of the United States. Indeed, the very worst possible state of affairs would be one wherein we "succeed" in convincing both the Soviets and ourselves that "Star Wars" would work. This is because as work proceeded on defense, the Soviets would be faced with a real incentive to preempt before the shield were in place.

Strategic defense has its appeals. Its supporters ask only that we give new technologies a chance. What they fail to understand is that the stability of nuclear deterrence rests upon mutual vulnerability. It follows that an ambitious program to prevent the other side's "assured destruction capability" is enormously *offensive*. This should already be obvious to everyone who remembers that the MIRVed (multiple independently targeted reentry vehicle) Soviet weapons that threaten us today were developed originally to penetrate an earlier generation of ABM (antiballistic missile) defenses.

President Reagan has said that because Star Wars will be entirely defensive, the Soviets have nothing to fear. But in this assessment he displays a near-total misunderstanding of nuclear deterrence. Significantly, if the Soviets were to embark upon the defensive system now being planned in Washington, the United States would respond with a greatly accelerated deployment of offensive missile systems—nuclear weapons that could reliably penetrate the Soviet shield.

The main problem with the president's reasoning is that it ignores Soviet uncertainty. Notwithstanding his assurances of peaceful U.S. intentions, there is little cause for complaisance in Moscow. From the Soviet perspective, everything points to U.S. flirtation with a disarming first strike, especially as our plan for strategic defense is coupled with the ongoing deployment of MX, Trident II, and Euromissiles—a deployment with distinctly counterforce, or war-fighting qualities.

The president has said that it is time to shift from deterrence to defense, but no such shift is possible. The development of Star Wars will never replace nuclear deterrence; it will merely destabilize it. The president has said that the Soviets need have no fears of a U.S. first strike. Everyone knows that the United States is "good" and the Soviet Union is "bad." But it doesn't look this way from the Soviet point of view:

- The Soviets see a United States that is the only country to have used nuclear weapons;
- the Soviets see a United States that has refused to renounce (as they have renounced) the right to first use of nuclear weapons;
- the Soviets see a United States that has refused to ratify and observe the SALT II Treaty and then has had the gall to accuse them of noncompliance;
- the Soviets see a United States that has surrounded their country with 572 new (Pershing II and ground-launched cruise) missiles.

The president has said that Star Wars can work and that the Soviets are less likely to attack if the United States has such defense, even if it is imperfect. Yet, according to all that we know about the logic of deterrence, Soviet judgment on whether or not to attack first will be contingent on (1) expectations of retaliatory destruction and (2) expectations of U.S. preemption.

If all U.S. cities were completely vulnerable, a rational Soviet adversary would never strike first unless it believed it could do so without suffering unacceptably damaging retaliation. Moreover, under such conditions the Soviets would have no cause for concern about U.S. preemption. Conversely, if all U.S. cities were completely defensible, the Soviets might decide to strike first if they believed they could do so without suffering assured destruction. Their concern over a U.S. first strike under such conditions would be enormous. Whether or not the Soviets believe they would gain from striking first will depend entirely on their views of U.S. intentions. Because Star Wars signals a search for defense, it suggests a greatly enhanced prospect of a U.S. first strike. Thus, it can only enlarge the chances that the Soviets will preempt.

President Reagan does not understand the calculus of nuclear deterrence. Recognizing that each side could "assuredly destroy" the other after absorbing a first strike, he concludes falsely that U.S. safety would be reinforced by strategic defense. But there are circumstances in which striking first would be the rational Soviet choice, however damaging the expected retaliation. These are circumstances in which the only perceived Soviet alternative to striking first is to be struck first. *Because U.S. defense may create these circumstances, Star Wars greatly undermines our national security.*

In the final analysis, many of those who favor Star Wars are driven by the visceral anti-Sovietism of the time. Unwilling to work through the complex logical arguments associated with nuclear strategy, they retreat to the vacant intuitions of armchair warriors, comforted not by wisdom but by dogma. Too often, they attempt to discredit the other side's position by invoking colorful metaphors and patriotic fervor.

Comprehensive Test Ban

Second, the time has come for a banning of all nuclear-weapons testing. Despite the 1963 Partial Test Ban Treaty, the 1973 Limited Test Ban Treaty, the 1974 Treaty on the Limitation of Underground Nuclear Weapon Tests, the 1974 Threshold Treaty, and the 1976 Treaty on Underground Nuclear Explosions for Peaceful Purposes, only a comprehensive test ban (CTB) can substantially inhibit further nuclear-weapons innovations. A comprehensive nuclear test ban would represent the fulfillment of a goal first outlined in the late 1950s. Recognizing this, the U.S. House of Representatives, early in 1986, passed a resolution (by a vote of 268 to 148) calling upon the president to resume talks on a comprehensive test ban treaty.

With a CTB treaty in place, parties would be inhibited from deploying untested weapons, an inhibition that would reduce first-strike fears and further undercut arguments for counterforce weapons and policies. Moreover, CTB would strengthen and complement other arms control agreements, eliminate environmental and health hazards associated with the testing of nuclear weapons, and reduce the enormously debilitating diversion of wealth that is an integral feature of current nuclear strategy. Significantly, most of the countries participating in the 1985 NPT Review Conference insisted upon a comprehensive test ban treaty.

No-First-Use Pledge

Third, reciprocating Soviet policy, the United States must take the declaratory step of renouncing first use of nuclear weapons. Regrettably, although a no-first-use pledge would be an important step in the process of de-legitimizing nuclear weapons, the United States continues to oppose such a measure. This opposition still stems from the NATO strategy of deterring a Soviet conventional attack with U.S. nuclear weapons. U.S. policy excludes the use of nuclear weapons as the first offensive move of war (a first strike), but does not exclude their retaliatory use to stave off defeat in a major conventional conflict.

A no-first-use pledge would be contrary to the rudiments of current U.S. nuclear deterrence strategy. To permit a renunciation of the first-use option, the United States would have to calculate that the expected benefits of such renunciation would outweigh the expected costs. To allow such a calculation, which would involve abandonment of the Euromissiles, the United States would have to undertake substantial efforts to upgrade conventional forces.[4] These efforts would be needed to preserve a sufficiently high nuclear threshold.

But why, we might ask, should the U.S. policy of first use appear threatening to the Soviets? After all, it has always been the official policy of the United States not to launch a first strike, that is, a nuclear strike as an initial, offensive move of war. Is there anything provocative in a nuclear strategy that does not exclude the *retaliatory* use of nuclear weapons to stave off defeat in a conventional conflict?

The answer to this question lies in the fact that, in actual practice, the distinctions between the first use of nuclear weapons and a nuclear first strike are likely to be meaningless. Once an adversary had committed an act of aggression, the United States would certainly characterize an intended nuclear response as a first use rather than as a first strike. Because the determination that an act of aggression had taken place would necessarily be made by the United States rather than by some specially constituted central arbiter, certain acts that are judged to be aggressive by the United States might be expected to warrant a U.S. nuclear response.

But doesn't the arbitrariness of the distinction between first use and first strike apply equally to Soviet strategy? Isn't that strategy as threatening to the United States as U.S. strategy is to the Soviets? The answer to this question is clearly "no," as the asymmetry in conventional forces between the two superpowers provides the Soviet Union with little real incentive to initiate an escalation to nuclear conflict.

Together with the consequences of U.S. inferiority in conventional forces, the U.S. policy of first use is especially unsettling to the Soviet Union because it (1) allows for rapid escalation to nuclear conflict; (2) allows for the possibility of disguising a first strike as a first use, either by deliberately creating conditions that lead to "acts of aggression" or by falsely alleging that such acts have taken place; and (3) joins with a targeting doctrine that focuses on Soviet strategic forces.

Joint Nuclear Freeze

The United States and the USSR must implement a freeze on nuclear arms.[5] Specifically, the superpowers should adopt a mutual freeze on the testing, production, and deployment of nuclear weapons and of missiles and new aircraft designed primarily to deliver nuclear weapons. Verifiable by highly reliable national technical means, this freeze should be followed by negotiations to codify the moratorium into a formal treaty. Procedurally these negotiations might follow the precedent of the 1958–1961 nuclear-weapons test moratorium, during which time testing was suspended while the United States, the USSR, and Great Britain negotiated a partial test ban treaty.

The freeze is an idea whose time has come. In a world where existing superpower arsenals of nuclear weapons are clearly adequate to the requirements of assured destruction, the continuation of the arms race can produce only instability. Rather than codify a condition of inferiority for the United States, a freeze would set the stage for success of associated arms control efforts, reduce the rationale for countervailing strategies of deterrence, and greatly reduce the threat of horizontal proliferation. Moreover, a freeze would be particularly susceptible to verification. This is because a freeze would mean a stop to all activities in any nuclear-weapons program. Whereas other attempts at arms control require monitoring a particular ceiling, verification of a freeze would require only detection of *any* missile or aircraft.

Indeed, viewed in cost/benefit terms, it is clear that the prospective security benefits that would accrue to the United States from a freeze would outweigh the costs even if some Soviet cheating were to take place. This is because such cheating would necessarily be on a very minor scale, whereas the overall effect of the freeze would be to initiate deescalatory processes and restore minimum deterrence. Why, then, does the Reagan administration reject the freeze? The answer seems to lie in its revised definition of deterrence, a definition that links success with the capacity to dominate escalation during a nuclear war and that is completely at variance with the alleged benefits of defense. The freeze is objectionable to the administration not because it would create the conditions under which the United States would be unable to devastate the Soviet Union after absorbing a first-strike attack, but because it would interfere with the capacity to wage nuclear war "rationally."

Nuclear-Weapon-Free Zones

Fourth, the superpowers must adopt an effective plan for nuclear-free zones. The concept of such zones has already received international legal expression in the Treaty for the Prohibition of Nuclear Weapons in Latin

America (the Treaty of Tlatelolco), which entered into force on April 22, 1968, and the two protocols to the treaty. Unlike two earlier treaties that seek to limit the spread of nuclear weapons into "pristine" areas—the Antarctic Treaty of 1961 and the Outer Space Treaty of 1967—the Latin American treaty concerns a populated area. The terms of the treaty include measures to prevent the type of deployment of nuclear weapons that led to the Cuban missile crisis, methods of verification by both the parties themselves and by their own regional organization, and IAEA safeguards on all nuclear materials and facilities under the jurisdiction of the parties. In the years ahead, the Treaty of Tlatelolco must become a model for imitation in other areas of the world. In the absence of universal respect for NPT commitments, nuclear-weapon-free zones offer an auspicious means of reducing the number of sources of superpower confrontation and conflict. A majority of states already supports the idea of nuclear-weapon-free zones.

We have seen that the superpowers, by restructuring their central strategic relationship along the lines of minimum deterrence, comprehensive test ban, no-first-use pledges, joint nuclear freeze, and nuclear-weapon-free zones, could offer the non-nuclear-weapons states a significant incentive not to proliferate. Additional incentives, however, would also be needed. Of these, the most important would be an understanding that nuclear weapons do not enhance the security of those states that still do not possess them. Although such a view would prove difficult to understand in a world committed to the principles of "realism," its essential truthfulness suggests some cause for optimism. This cause might be heightened by the recognition on the part of prospective proliferants of the burdensome costs associated with a military nuclear program and by offering superpower security assurances to non-nuclear allies.

The nuclear powers might also contribute to the cause of nonproliferation with a pledge not to use nuclear weapons against non-nuclear-weapons-states. Such a pledge, if it were generally credible, could contribute to the understanding that nonacquisition of nuclear weapons promotes safety. For example, accession to such a pledge by Israel, a near-nuclear power, might provide incentives to certain Arab states not to go nuclear.[6]

In conjunction with these measures, the IAEA must be granted greater authority to inspect nuclear facilities, search for clandestine stockpiles, and pursue stolen nuclear materials. Ultimately, such authority must be extended to all nuclear facilities of all non-nuclear-weapons states. Without such a tightening of IAEA safeguards, a number of non-nuclear-weapons states can be expected to calculate that the benefits of nonproliferation are exceeded by the costs.

The IAEA must also be allowed to enforce more stringent requirements for protection of weapons-usable nuclear materials in transport between nations. In this connection, the Convention on the Physical Protection of Nuclear Materials, which has not yet come into force because of a lack of accessions, should be ratified promptly. This convention, although chiefly directed toward protection of international transfers of peaceful nuclear materials, does include certain requirements that also apply within nations.

The strengthening and expanding of IAEA safeguards and functions is essential to nonproliferation and the avoidance of nuclear terrorism.[7] These goals can also be served by an improved international capability for gathering covert intelligence. In the future, many of the intelligence capabilities that now rest entirely with national governments will need to be pooled and coordinated.

A final arena in which the nonproliferation regime can be improved is that of nuclear export policy.[8] This is the case because access to a nuclear-weapons capability now depends largely on the policies of a small group of supplier states. In years ahead, these states—which carry on international commerce in nuclear facilities, nuclear technology, and nuclear materials—will have to improve and coordinate their export policies.

The heart of the problem, of course, is the fact that nuclear exports, although they may contribute to the spread of nuclear weapons, are a lucrative market for a supplier state. Moreover, in certain exchanges, such exports are also a crucial political lever in assuring access to oil. Recognizing the conflict in objectives between nonproliferation and a nuclear export market, the International Atomic Energy Agency, Euratom, and the Treaty on the Non-Proliferation of Nuclear Weapons impose obligations on nuclear exports concerning the development of nuclear explosives. Article 1 of the NPT pledges the signatories "not in any way to assist, encourage, or induce any non-nuclear weapon State to manufacture or otherwise acquire nuclear weapons or other nuclear explosive devices." At the same time, Article 4 of the NPT ensures that "all parties to the Treaty undertake to facilitate, and have the right to participate in, the fullest possible exchange of equipment, materials, and scientific and technological information for the peaceful uses of nuclear energy." In this connection, unilateral U.S conditions on U.S. nuclear material exports are imposed by the Nuclear Non-Proliferation Act of 1978 (NNPA).

To avoid the hazards of a worldwide plutonium economy, the United States and other suppliers must press ahead with efforts to halt the diffusion of national plutonium reprocessing and enrichment facilities.[9] If at all possible, prohibitions on the export of sensitive technologies should be carried out on a multilateral basis. Although it should be generally understood that it is in every supplier state's best interests to inhibit the spread of technologies with serious proliferation hazards,[10] such an understanding is always contingent on the expectation of restraint by every other supplier state.

What this means, in essence, is that all supplier states can be expected to comply with the requirements of a common nuclear export policy only if they all believe that such compliance will be generally observed. From the standpoint of creating an effective consensus on nuclear exports, the problem is one of securing compliance as long as each supplier state is uncertain about the reciprocal compliance of all other supplier states. Unless each supplier state believes that its own willingness to comply is generally paralleled, it is apt to calculate that the benefits of compliance are exceeded by the costs.

Needed to relieve this problem are: (1) an adequate system for verification of compliance with common nuclear export policies; and (2) a system of sanctions for noncompliance in which the costs of departure from such policies are so great as to outweigh the expected benefits of export revenues. In practice, the victory of nonproliferation objectives over commercial goals will depend upon the willingness and capacity of the nuclear supplier states to exert serious political and economic pressures upon recalcitrant colleagues to conform with common policies. In the absence of such willingness and capacity, supplier states are apt to pay closer attention to their balance of payments and petroleum problems than to their long-term security interests. Such priorities would have enormously corrosive effects on the nonproliferation regime.

In the control of nuclear exports, sanctions can play a vital part in affecting the decisions of recipient states. Because nonproliferation is an integral part of the plan to prevent nuclear terrorism, such sanctions must be considered to be targeted against states that support or at least tolerate the prospect of such terrorism. In this connection, such sanctions are already a part of U.S. agreements for nuclear cooperation with certain other countries; of the IAEA statute; and of the Foreign Assistance Act as amended by the International Assistance and Arms Export Control Act of 1976. The specific sanctions in these cases include suspension of agreements and the return of transferred materials; curtailment or suspension of assistance provided by the IAEA; suspension from membership in the IAEA; and ineligibility for economic, military, or security assistance. At the same time, selective U.S. support for terrorists of its own (support generated by the presumed imperatives of the Reagan Doctrine) could undermine the effectiveness of sanctions.

As long as the world system fails to provide vulnerable states with a reasonable assurance of protection against nuclear attack, such states will continue to rely on the remedy of self-help. Understood in terms of the June 1981 Israeli air strike against the Iraqi nuclear reactor near Baghdad, this suggests that the real adversaries of nonproliferation are not states like Israel, which may have no effective alternative to preemption, but rather states such as France, Italy, Canada, Switzerland, and West Germany, which have undertaken imprudent sales of nuclear technologies and materials to unstable countries.

The United States must also bear certain responsibility for nonproliferation failures. In this connection, not only has it failed to dissuade its allies from their shortsighted excursions in nuclear commerce, it has also reversed efforts by the Ford and Carter administrations to defer reprocessing of civilian fuel and the use of plutonium here and abroad. Moreover, the Reagan administration has supplied Argentina with nuclear assistance, most recently in the form of 143 tons of heavy water, despite that country's refusal to comply with international nonproliferation norms. On November 18, 1983, Argentina announced that it was now capable of enriching uranium, a capability that gives it direct access to atomic bomb material.

To improve its policies to halt proliferation, the United States must first begin to comply with its own nuclear export and plutonium-use standards. Although the United States should continue as a nuclear supplier to reliable national customers, it should refuse to supply states that reject essential safeguards or pursue plutonium economies. As Paul Leventhal has pointed out, "This necessarily involves linking U.S. nonproliferation objectives to a wide range of political, economic and security issues with other nations, and not confining non-proliferation discussions to the narrow area of nuclear commerce, as is now largely the case."[11]

As with all of the other elements of its foreign policy, the Reagan administration's subordination of nonproliferation objectives to alleged considerations of power—in this case a repair of relations strained by U.S. support for Britain in the Falklands war—reflects the primacy of realpolitik. The administration should not be surprised, therefore, when its intelligence surveys reveal that thirty-one states, many of them engaged in longstanding regional disputes, will be able to produce nuclear weapons by the year 2000.[12] Such findings are the inevitable result of misconceived judgments of national interest.

At the same time, too much faith cannot be invested in the rules and procedures of the nonproliferation regime. In its existing form, the Non-Proliferation Treaty, which was reviewed for the third time in 1985, does little to assure worried states about the intentions of adversary states.[13] To attract signatories, the NPT trades off effectiveness for obeisance to national sovereignty. Although 133 states had acceded to the treaty by July 1986, a number of states with substantial nuclear power programs had yet to accept it.[14] A state can withdraw at any time after ninety days notice and may choose its own inspectors. Moreover, the NPT limits the International Atomic Energy Agency to bring to public notice any breaches of the treaty. It does not bestow upon the IAEA the power to sanction such breaches. Without the authority to look for undeclared material or for clandestine operations, the IAEA in effect conducts a limited accounting operation.

In the final analysis, however, even a greatly strengthened nonproliferation regime would be inadequate to the task at hand. Although such a regime, assisted by a more vigorous IAEA utilizing surveillance cameras and automatic fuel-rod counting machines, would certainly be welcome, a much more basic kind of change is needed. This is a change in the underlying dynamic of fear and suspicion, a dynamic that can ultimately overcome any attempts at mechanical or technical solutions. The problem was understood best, perhaps, by the remarkable Trappist monk and scholar, Thomas Merton:

> When there is a deep, simple, all-embracing love of man, of the created world of living and inanimate things, then there will be respect for life, for freedom, for truth, for justice and there will be humble love of God. But where there is no love of man, no love of life, then make all the laws you want, all the edicts and treaties, issue all the anathemas; set up all the safeguards and inspections, fill the air with spying satellites, and hang cameras on the moon. As long as you see your fellow man as a being essentially to be feared, mistrusted, hated and destroyed, there cannot be peace on earth.[15]

Nonproliferation and International Political Power

Ultimately, the effectiveness of nonproliferation as a means to prevent nuclear terrorism will depend upon a cooperative effort by the United States and the Soviet Union to control limited aspects of their respective alliance systems.[16] Moreover, it will depend upon an extension of such superpower control to all prospective proliferator states that fall under the orbit of U.S. or Soviet influence. Although such a statement seems to exhibit characteristics of a new elitism, the effect of such control would be to bolster world order rather than primacy. Rather than reassert an earlier form of duopolistic domination, a selective tightening of bipolarity in world power processes could significantly enhance the promise of nonproliferation. This is the case because a tightening of superpower control over allies and other states would limit the freedom of action these states have to go nuclear. The tighter the dualism of power, the greater the ability of the superpowers to assure broad compliance with nonproliferation goals and thereby prevent nuclear terrorism.

An important part of the nonproliferation/nuclear-terrorism problem, therefore, is the control of too large a number of independent national wills. Such control is an instance of the more general problem of decision that arises when the benefits of common action are contingent upon the expectation that all parties will cooperate. Nonproliferation efforts will always be problematic to the extent that they rely upon volitional compliance. They may, however, be successful if the superpowers move with determination to assure the compliance of other states with the NPT and its associated norms and restrictions.

The impending spread of nuclear weapons is fueled not by madness or malignant motives, but by basically well-intentioned persons who find such weapons essential to national security.[17] To prevent the spread of such weapons, therefore, we must not seek to root out the bad from the good, but to convince everyone that going nuclear would be counterproductive. In principle, this should not be difficult to do. As we have already seen, no strategy for security could possibly be less realistic than what is called realism. Nonetheless, old ideas, however time-dishonored, do not die easily, and the creation of a new system of world security will require a species of fortitude that borders on the sublime.

To begin, the scaffolding of the present nonproliferation regime will have to be strengthened by a restructuring of the central strategic relationship of the superpowers, an improved nonproliferation treaty, the strengthening of IAEA safeguards and functions, the expansion of nuclear-free zones, and common and effective nuclear export policies. After this scaffolding has been firmed up, it will be necessary for the superpowers to cooperate more self-consciously in pursuit of nonproliferation goals. At a critical juncture during such cooperation, the Soviet Union and the United States will have to extend their own previously worked-out principles of nuclear-war avoidance to the rest of the family of nations. These principles, of course, will rest on a new understanding of national interests—one that recognizes the futility of military competition and the imperative of working for the survival of the system as a whole.

Will it work? Can humankind be expected to grasp hold of this calculus of potentiality, reaffirming the sovereignty of reason over the forces of disintegration? Can nations be expected to tear down the walls of competitive power struggles and replace them with the permeable membranes of spirited cooperation?

Probably not! But there is surely no other way. So long as individual states continue to identify their own security with the acquisition of destructive weaponry, they will have only war. The Talmud tells us,

"The dust from which the first man was made was gathered in all the corners of the world." By moving toward a new planetary identity, the peoples of earth can begin to build bridges over the most dangerous abyss they have ever known. Hopefully, even in this absurd theater of modern world politics, human beings will choose life rather than death. Stripped of false hopes, and without illusion, humanity may yet stare at the specter of nuclear terrorism and nuclear holocaust with passionate attention and experience the planetary responsibility that will bring liberation.

We began this inquiry into strategies of counter–nuclear terrorism with a brief synopsis of Kafka's novella *The Metamorphosis*. The story is pertinent to our concerns as a parable that illustrates the options at hand: summoning the locksmith (improved physical security) and sending for the doctor (improved behavioral measures). Both options must be pursued vigorously, imaginatively, internationally, and simultaneously. At the moment, however, only the first option is being taken seriously. The second continues to be widely ignored. This situation is as absurd as the literary genre that springs from Kafka's oblique way of regarding experience. To reach and sustain a more hopeful situation, one in which the human race is granted a functional dispensation from nuclear terrorism, nations will have to place ever greater emphasis on behavioral countermeasures.

Internationally, as we shall soon see, such measures must include special patterns of cooperation between like-minded governments, sanctions against states that sponsor or support terrorism, and a fuller application of international legal norms. With respect to international law, greater respect must be accorded to the principle of "extradite or prosecute"; states must respect the definition of aggression approved by the General Assembly in 1974; and terrorists must come to be regarded by all states as "common enemies of mankind." Taken together, such measures could severely limit the likelihood of nuclear terrorism.

However, to be genuinely promising, such measures will require a far more sweeping transformation of world politics, one in which all states renounce mindless "realism" in favor of planetary consciousness. To begin this transformation, states must arrive at the understanding that fostering terrorism can never be in their long-term best interests. The unity of states against terrorism is the essential precondition for avoiding terrorist nuclear violence. Such unity, therefore, is also an essential requirement of a secure world order.

A few years after the Declaration of Independence, the Continental Congress adopted as a motto on the Great Seal of the United States a phrase of Virgil's, *Novus Ordo Seclorum* ("a new age beginning"). In a world imperiled by multiple dangers of nuclear violence, it is time for such a motto to be applied internationally. Nuclear terrorism, like the other principal paths to nuclear catastrophe in world politics, is threatening largely because of the uninterrupted primacy of militaristic nationalism among states. Its terrible possiblities, including nuclear war, can be avoided only when states escape from their own misconceptions of self-interest. To witness a new age beginning among all states, citizens of the world must work to remove these misconceptions, substituting the dignity of cooperation for the degradation of mortal competition. In so doing, they can create an intellectual and spiritual foundation upon which the move to planetization may be actualized.

The U.S. Obligation

In one of his books, Jorge Luis Borges speaks of a time in the future when politics will disappear and politicians will go on to become either comedians or faith healers (because that is what they are most suited to do). For the moment, however, such time is not yet at hand, and politicians will have to be taken seriously. This is true for both the United States and the Soviet Union.

In the United States, obsessive anti-Sovietism is a strategy for public manipulation. Less an ideology than the absence of an ideal, it is exploited by cynical political elites to displace private anguish and to sustain existing patterns of power. A surreal spectrum of clichés masquerading as serious thought, it distorts patriotic fervor and points unambiguously toward war. Left unchecked, it will leave only crushed bones as mementos.

The problem has been recognized with particular insight by George Konra'd, one of Eastern Europe's most distinguished writers:

> In point of fact, it is not ideologies that contend today, nor is it systems like capitalism and communism. Anyone who believes that two systems and two ideologies are pitted against each other today has fallen victim to the secularized metaphysics of our civilization, which looks for a duel between God and Satan in what is, after all, only a game. Russians and Americans—their political classes, that is—circle each other in the ring. Each of the two world heavyweight champions would like to show he is the strongest in the world; they are playing a game with each other whose paraphernalia include nuclear missiles. Yet it is impossible to construct from the Soviet-American conflict an ideological dichotomy along whose axis the values of our continent can be ranged. The antitheses which fill our mental horizon—capitalism versus state socialism, democracy versus totalitarianism, market economy versus planned economy—are forced mythologies which the intelligentsias of East and West either confuse with reality or else, being aware that they are not very precise appelations, seek to square with the real facts.[18]

The underlying point of contention between the superpowers is therefore not ideological or economic, but a groundless rhetoric reinforced by self-serving elites. Indeed, the rivalry between the United States and the Soviet Union, once spawned and sustained by genuine considerations of purpose and power, is now essentially a contrivance, nurtured by their respective leadership bodies who have more in common with each other than with their respective populations.

In what is perhaps the greatest single irony of modern world politics, these elites and their "defense community" handmaidens are *true* allies, supporting each other while they undermine the security of both countries. As allies, of course, they don't recognize their mutual support structure and interdependence. There is nothing conspiratorial about their relationship—but it exists nonetheless. In their mutual relationship, the defense communities of the superpowers coexist in a condition of symbiosis. Each is essential to the health and survival of the other. But in their relationship with their respective societies and with the world as a whole, they are parasitic, drawing from that organism that is humanity the very life blood of a species approaching extinction.

To ensure that such circumstances remain as they are, the two communities have developed and promoted an arcane nuclear theology, a scriptural system of norms and beliefs upheld by a priesthood of "experts." As those who exist apart from this priesthood are judged incapable of offering meaningful criticism of the new faith in "nuclearism," objections are ruled out of order. "Do not dare to challenge," we are warned. The authorities know best.

But what are the declared foundations of this new theology? Above all, we are reminded, they rest on science. Vitalized by hard data and by the most impressive computer technology, they are advanced by "professionals" who will brook no interference by laypersons. But the toughminded disposition of these strategists does not imply understanding. As Hannah Arendt noted some time ago, the new priesthood is cold-blooded enough to consider discomforting thoughts, but in such consideration it does not really *think*. In Arendt's words:

Instead of indulging in such an old-fashioned, uncomputerizable activity, they reckon with the consequences of certain hypothetically assumed constellations without, however, being able to test their hypotheses against actual occurrences. The logical flaw in these hypothetical constructions of future events is always the same: what first appears as a hypothesis—with or without its implied alternatives, according to the level of sophistication— turns immediately, usually after a few paragraphs, into a "fact," which then gives birth to a whole string of similar non-facts, with the result that the purely speculative character of the whole enterprise is forgotten. Needless to say, this is not science, but pseudo-science.[19]

There is another element of this new theology, one that makes it even more resistant to challenge. Current U.S. nuclear strategy does not discover all of its authority in science. Its rationale is also embedded in quasi-religious fantasies of struggle between the Sons of Light and the Sons of Darkness.

Dostoevsky understood that killing is often distasteful, but that the distaste may be swallowed if it is essential to true heroism. And what greater heroism can there be than to take up arms in the Final Battle Against Evil. By characterizing its competition with the Soviet Union in starkly apocalyptic terms, the Reagan administration now prods us to even greater "loyalty." In a world where the United States can assert its own sacredness, there must be no serious challenge to public authority, a challenge that would represent not democratic dissent but blasphemy.

We see, therefore, that the requirements of *real* political action—moves by already conscious individuals to encourage new and far-reaching sources of self-worth that are unsullied by statecraft—will be hard to satisfy. Not only will these requirements include an illumination of our fragile bases of self-worth in a world dominated by superpower competition, but also a full exposure of the misuses of science and the perversions of faith. As inhabitants of a multistate world, Americans must learn to understand that nuclearism is not Reason and that our enemy is not Satan. With such an understanding, we might still reverse the obscene transfer of both science and the sacred to our technology of annihilation, a reversal that would signal the triumph of personhood over the herd and, ultimately, of life over death.

In the final analysis, U.S. safety from nuclear terrorism will depend upon our ability to renounce an obsessive anti-Sovietism. Determining every action from the standpoint of its probable impact on U.S.-Soviet rivalry, the Reagan administration generates policies that nurture anti-Americanism. As we have seen, foremost among these policies are, first, support of "authoritarian" regimes and, second, violent opposition to "totalitarian" regimes (the Reagan Doctrine).

U.S. support for authoritarian regimes in the interest of countering Soviet power in entirely misconceived. Such support may generate terrorism against the United States (1) by insurgents fighting U.S. backed regimes; and (2) by the successor governments that harbor ill will toward the United States for its prior indifference to human rights. It may even generate domestic terrorism by U.S. citizens who might be driven to violence by the Reagan administration's indifference to international law and to the historic political traditions of the United States. An example would be the Sanctuary Movement in the United States, radicalized by U.S. willingness to admit refugees from Cuba and Nicaragua while turning away those fleeing from El Salvador, Guatemala, and Chile. Anguished by a policy that treats South Africa, South Korea, and Paraguay as part of the free world (a category that recently included Haiti and the Philippines as well) but regards Angola and Nicaragua as "captive nations," individual Americans may turn increasingly to terrorist violence. Should this happen, it is likely to flow not from the sentiments of ordinary criminality, but rather from an interpretation of the Nuremberg obligation to resist crimes of state.

But what about Haiti and the Philippines? For the moment, it would appear that prior U.S. support of the Duvalier and Marcos tyrannies has produced nothing in the manner of anti-U.S. terrorism. Although the Reagan administration cut its ties to these "authoritarian" regimes only because they had become ineffectual (and not because they had been barbarous), the generally accepted impression of U.S. involvement is that of a "liberator."

Significantly, Haiti and the Philippines are not Iran and Nicaragua. For now, the successor governments are on "our side." Yet, the long-term effects of U.S.-backed authoritarianism in these countries are still unclear, and it is altogether likely that their governments will be replaced or undermined by leftist elements strongly opposed to the United States. If that should happen, these elements might spawn substantial forms of anti-U.S. terrorism.

What about South Korea? In that country the opposition is demanding a constitutional amendment on direct presidential elections in 1988, the year President Chun Doo Hwan has said he will leave the office he took over in a military coup six years ago. Will the United States continue to back Chun Doo Hwan as an essential bulwark of the free world? If the United States does, can it count on the same *short-term* success it experienced in the Philippines? If not, we might expect a successor government that will support anti-U.S. terrorism.

U.S. military support to overthrow "totalitarian" (Marxist, pro-Soviet) regimes—the Reagan Doctrine—represents a major incentive for anti-U.S. terrorism. Lacking any foundation in international law (which treats such support as prima facie instances of aggression), it will inevitably fail. Nicaragua and Angola are not Grenada. During the next year, opposition in those countries to contra and Unita rebels (who are characterized by international law as terrorists because of their repeated violation of the humanitarian rules of war) may include counterterrorism attacks against the United States or U.S. personnel and interests abroad. Moreover, opposition in certain other countries (e.g., the rebels in El Salvador) may join in such attacks.

By acting according to the Reagan Doctrine, the United States chooses to "destabilize" Nicaragua and Angola while maintaining its support of El Salvador, Chile, and South Africa. Yet, according to every independent standard of human-rights abuse, the practices of our allies are vastly more repressive than those of our enemies. Again, the justification lies in geopolitics, in the presumed imperative to counter the Soviet Union at all costs. Beginning in 1945, this imperative occasioned freedom and favors for Nazi war criminals. Today it sustains thugs as the "moral equal of our Founding Fathers." Because the world is not blind to such rhetorical manipulations of truth (for example, Bishop Tutu's repeated promise to "remember America" when apartheid is overthrown), the result of the Reagan Doctrine can only include increased instances of terrorism against the United States.

In the end, to reduce the risk of anti-U.S. terrorism, including nuclear terrorism, the United States has only one effective option: to reduce its all-consuming rivalry with the Soviet Union. Although the USSR has played its part in creating and sustaining this rivalry, and although certain terrorist grievances against the United States have nothing to do with obsessive U.S. anti-Sovietism, the overriding hazard lies in U.S. leaders' narrow vision of world order and conflict. Convinced that every international interaction is a mere manifestation of superpower competition, U.S. leaders embrace policies that consistently injure U.S. interests and ideals at the same time. Proud of their ethical double standard because it is compelled by struggle with an "evil empire,"[20] these leaders make all forms of anti-U.S. terrorism increasingly probable.

5

Softening the Adversary: Behavioral Strategies

Even if sophisticated physical security measures are extended throughout the world, they will not be adequate for the task at hand. It is not enough to safeguard strategic special nuclear materials and nuclear weapons to prevent nuclear terrorism. Nor can the United States expect immunity from nuclear terrorism by undertaking necessary changes in foreign policy. To augment physical safeguards and policy improvements, we must create a *behavioral* strategy, one that is directed toward producing certain changes in the decisional calculi of terrorist groups and their sponsor states.

Such a behavioral strategy must be based upon a sound understanding of the risk calculations of terrorists. Until we understand the special terrorist stance on the balance of risks that can be taken in world politics, we will not be able to identify an appropriate system of sanctions. Although terrorists are typically apt to tolerate higher levels of death and injury than are states, there *is* a threshold beyond which certain costs become intolerable. To understand this threshhold, we must first recall that there is no such thing as "the terrorist mind." Rather, there are many terrorists minds, a great variety of ideas, methods, visions, and objectives. To seek a uniformly applicable strategy of counter–nuclear terrorism, therefore, would represent the height of folly.

Contrariwise, in spite of the obvious heterogeneity that characterizes modern terrorism, it would be immensely impractical to formulate myriad different strategies that are tailored to particular groups. What must be established is a limited and manageable number of basic strategies that are formed according to the principal types of terrorist group behavior. By adopting this means of "blueprinting" effective counter-nuclear-terrorist action, policymakers can be presented with a decision-making taxonomy in which strategies are differentiated according to the particular category of risk calculation involved.

This is not to suggest that each terrorist group comprises individuals who exhibit the same pattern of behavior, the same stance on the balance of risks that can be taken in pursuit of particular preferences. Rather, each terrorist group is made up, in varying degrees, of persons with disparate motives. Because it is essential, from the point of view of creating the necessary decisional taxonomy, that each terrorist *group* be categorized according to a particular type of risk calculation, the trick is to identify and evaluate the leadership strata of each terrorist group in order to determine the predominant ordering of preferences.

In terms of actually mounting an effective counter-nuclear-terrorist strategy, therefore, governments must organize their activities according to the following sequence of responsibilities:

1. Appraise the terrorist group under scrutiny for the purpose of identifying leadership elements.
2. Appraise the leadership elements for the purpose of identifying predominant patterns of risk-calculation.
3. Examine the decision-making taxonomy for the purpose of identifying the appropriate type of counter-nuclear-terrorist strategy, that is, the strategy that corresponds with the identified pattern of risk calculation.

In so organizing their counter-nuclear-terrorist activities, governments can begin to develop a rationally conceived behavioral technology that distinguishes contingencies of reinforcement according to the particular type of terrorists involved. To deal effectively with the prospective problem of nuclear terrorism, it is essential to correlate deterrent and remedial measures with the preference orderings and modus operandi of the particular terrorist group(s) in question.

Examples of the Theory

For example, if a terrorist group displaying the self-sacrificing value system of certain Palestinian or Shia zealots were to threaten nuclear violence, it would be inappropriate to base deterrence on threats of physically punishing acts of retaliation. Here, negative physical sanctions, unless they are devastating enough to ensure destruction of the group itself, are bound to be ineffective. Indeed, such sanctions might even have the effect of a stimulus. Instead of orthodox threats of punishment, deterrence in this case should be based upon threats that promise to obstruct preferences that the terrorist group values even more highly than physical safety.[1]

Such threats, therefore, should be directed at convincing terrorists that the resort to nuclear violence would mitigate against their political objectives. To support such threats, steps would probably have to be taken to convince the terrorists that higher-order acts of violence are apt to generate broad-based repulsion rather than support.[2] As long as the threatened act of nuclear violence stems from propagandistic motives, terrorists who associate such violence with unfavorable publicity may be inclined to less-violent strategies.

Deterrence in this case might also be based upon the promise of rewards. Such a strategy of "positive sanctions" has been left out of current studies of counterterrorism; yet, it may prove to be one of the few potentially worthwhile ways of affecting the decisional calculi of terrorist groups with self-sacrificing value systems.[3] Of course, in considering whether this sort of strategy is appropriate in particular situations,[4] governments will have to decide whether the expected benefits that accrue from avoiding nuclear terrorism are great enough to outweigh the prospective costs associated with the promised concessions.[5]

For another example, we may consider the case of a terrorist group that exhibits a preference ordering very much like that of an ordinary criminal band; that is, its actions are dictated largely by incentives of material gain, however much these incentives are rationalized in terms of political objectives.[6] If such a terrorist group were to threaten nuclear violence, it would be as inappropriate to base deterrence on threats of political failure or negative public reception as it would be to threaten self-sacrificing ideologues with personal harm. Rather, deterrence in this case should be based largely upon the kinds of threats that are used to counter orthodox criminality.

This is not to suggest, however, that threats of physically punishing retaliation will always be productive in dealing with this type of terrorist group. Even though this particular type, unlike the self-sacrificing variety considered in the first example, is apt to value personal safety in its ordering of preferences, threats to impair this safety may be misconceived. Indeed, a great deal of sophisticated conceptual analysis and experimental evidence now seems to indicate that, in certain cases, the threat of physical punishment may actually prove counterproductive.[7] Contrary to the widely held conventional wisdom on the matter, taking a hard-line approach toward terrorists may only reinforce antagonism and intransigence. Recent experience indicates that physical retaliation against terrorists often causes only a shift in the selection of targets and a more protracted pattern of violence and aggression. The threat of physical punishment against terrorists is apt to generate high levels of anger that effectively raise the threshold of acceptable suffering. This is the case because anger can modify usual cost/benefit calculations, overriding the inhibitions ordinarily associated with anticipated punishment.

We have thus far limited the discussion of negative sanctions to physical punishment. However, there is considerable evidence that *all kinds* of negative sanctions—economic as well as physical—stiffen rather than diminish terrorist resistance. Whatever the nature of negative sanctions, they appear to generate anger that causes terrorists to value retaliation (or counterretaliation, whichever the case may be) more highly than the objectives that have given rise to terrorist activity in the first place.

For a third example, we may consider the case of a terrorist group that exhibits a primary concern for achieving one form or another of political objective, but that lacks a self-sacrificing value system. If this sort of terrorist group were to threaten nuclear violence, it would be appropriate to base deterrence on a suitable combination of all of the negative and positive sanctions discussed thus far. This means that steps should be taken to convince the group that (1) nuclear violence would mitigate against its political objectives, (2) certain concessions would be granted in exchange for restraint from nuclear violence,[8] and (3) certain physically punishing or otherwise negative acts of retaliation would be meted out if nuclear violence were undertaken.

In deciding upon what, exactly, constitutes a suitable configuration of sanctions, governments will have to be especially discriminating in their manner of brandishing threats of physical punishment. It is worth noting that threats of mild punishment may have a greater deterrent effect than threats of severe punishment. From the vantage point of the terrorist group's particular baseline of expectations, such threats—when threats of severe punishment are expected—may even appear to have positive qualities. Catching the terrorist group by surprise, such threat behavior is also less likely to elicit the high levels of anger and intractability that tend to override the inhibiting factor of expected punishment. Moreover, the threat of mild punishment is less likely to support the contention of official repression, a contention that is often a vital part of terrorist group strategies for success.[9]

In reference to the actual promise of rewards as an instrument of deterrence, governments may find it worthwhile to consider whether a selected number of particular concessions would produce a gainful net effect. In other words, recognizing that threats of severe punishment produce rationality-impairing stress, which in turn produces greater resistance rather than compliance, governments may discover that the promise of rewards communicates feelings of sympathy and concern, which in turn diminish terrorist resistance. With such an understanding, governments may begin to delimit the particular concessions that they are prepared to make.

A fourth and final example that illustrates the need to correlate deterrent and situational measures with particular preference orderings centers on the case of terrorist groups spurred on by the need for spectacular self-assertion. From the standpoint of preventing nuclear violence, this type of terrorist group presents the greatest problems. Faced with terrorist groups who long to act out ritualistic urgings, governments are confronted with genuine psychopaths and sociopaths. Clearly, as the preference that would need to be obstructed in this case is neither political success nor personal profit but the violent act itself, and as personal safety is unlikely to figure importantly in the terrorist risk calculation, deterrence of nuclear terrorism must be abandoned altogether as a viable strategy. Instead, all preventive measures must concentrate upon limiting the influence of such terrorists within their particular groups and maintaining a safe distance between such terrorists and the instruments of higher-order weapons technologies.

If the apparent danger is great enough, governments may feel compelled to resort to a no-holds-barred counterterrorist campaign. In such cases, governments must be aware that the inclination to escalate violence would signify the erosion of power. As Hannah Arendt has pointed out, violence and power are opposites. Where the latter is in jeopardy, the former is increased.[10] Understood in terms of antiterrorism measures, this suggests that the imprudent escalation of violence by public authorities can destroy power. Taken to its outermost limits, such escalation can lead to rule by sheer violence and the substitution of official terror for insurgent terror.

The Problem of Civil Liberties

In the preceding examples, some of the prospective sanctions available to counter-nuclear-terrorist strategists entail measures that might be injurious to such values as social justice and human rights within states. Of special interest in this connection are options involving (1) a total, no-holds-barred military-type assault designed to eradicate the terrorist group(s) altogether; and/or (2) a protracted, counterterrorist campaign utilizing such "classical" methods as informers, infiltrators, counterterrorist squads, assassinations, agents provocateurs, and selected raids.

The first option, however effective it might be, is apt to be most destructive of essential citizen rights. Hence, governments contemplating such an option must pay close attention to the necessary trade-off between efficacy and liberty that is involved. Because this option would almost certainly be repugnant to the most deeply held values of liberal, democratic societies, governments, before resorting to this option, would have to be convinced that its prospective benefits were great enough to outweigh its probable costs. In fact, short of its use at the situational level where higher-order acts of terrorist violence have already taken place, it is unlikely that this option will be taken seriously in democratic states. Rather, we are likely to see its routine adoption only by the world's most blatantly authoritarian, antidemocratic regimes.

This no-holds-barred military option is problematic for another reason. Not only might it incite fears of military/police repression among certain sectors of the population, it might also confer a genuine combatant status upon the terrorists. As a result, the terrorist group(s) would more likely acquire the cast of an underdog army than that of a lawless insurgency.

The second option is also apt to score high marks on the efficacy dimension, but its effects on essential citizen rights need not be as injurious. This is not to suggest that a protracted counterterrorist campaign utilizing classical methods of apprehension and punishment would necessarily be any less repulsive to decent, democratic societies, but that such a campaign might be conducted on a comparatively less-visible and clandestine basis. An additional virtue of such quiet operations would be the avoidance of sympathy-generating publicity for the terrorist group(s).

In the final analysis, the problem of conflicting values that emerges from the consideration of harsh deterrent countermeasures can be resolved only by careful comparison of the costs and benefits involved. In the absence of such a comparison, civil liberties might be curtailed under conditions far less threatening than nuclear terrorism. A good example of this is Canadian Prime Minister Trudeau's response to Front de Liberation Quebecois (FLQ) tactics of bombing and assassination in 1970. Taking steps to put his government on a genuine wartime footing against its internal insurgents, Trudeau invoked the War Measures Act on October 16, 1970, authorizing the government to do anything "it deems necessary for the security, defense, peace, order, and welfare of Canada." These steps were defended by the prime minister in his "total war" message to the country two days earlier: "There are a lot of bleeding hearts around who just don't like to see people with helmets and guns. All I can say is, go on and bleed, but it is more important to keep law and order in the society than to be worried about weak-kneed people . . . I think society must take every means at its disposal to defend itself against the emergence of a parallel power which defies the elected power in this country."

Canada is, of course, like the United States, a country that regards the protection of civil liberties as a fundamental principle of government.

Yet, in 1970, in response to a relatively low-risk crisis situation, it adopted short-run measures so sweeping that they removed basic liberties from the citizenry. It goes without saying, therefore, that the threat to civil liberties posed by nuclear terrorism in other, less democratic societies, is very real and must be taken seriously. In such societies, the line between underreaction and overreaction is unlikely to be walked with scrupulous concern. In general, the optimal counter-nuclear-terrorist strategy is one in which effective counteraction leaves the prevailing network of citizen rights and privileges unimpaired. Barring this possibility, however, the requirements of effective strategies[11] should be tempered by concern for those freedoms that are assured by humanitarian international law.[12]

In reference to the two options just outlined, it would be better for civil liberties if their sanctioning methods could be replaced altogether by the use of positive sanctions, moderate, ad hoc acts of physical punishment, efforts at underscoring the orthodox criminality of terrorist activities, and sustained efforts to convince terrorists that higher-order violence would be counterproductive to their objectives. Indeed, it would surely be a good idea for counter-nuclear-terrorist planners to begin to exploit the psychological warfare tactics set down in Sun Tzu's *The Book of War* in the fifth century B.C. If we recognize that in most cases, terrorist violence is not an end in itself, but an instrument for achieving desired personal/social/political change, we will see that certain terrorist groups might be deterred from nuclear violence to the extent that they believe such violence to be self-defeating. Unlike our first and second options, such tactics would recognize the primacy of ends over means in the preference orderings of most terrorist groups, and exploit this recognition by the establishment of reasoned countermeasures.

Such tactics, however, are intrinsically ill-suited to dealing with terrorist groups for whom higher-order acts of destruction are ends in themselves. In dealing with such groups, the first and second options may circumscribe the government's only means of defending the citizens in its charge. It follows that in such cases, the exigencies of survival may have to take precedence over the claims of libertarian values.

The Decision-making Taxonomy

The following taxonomy identifies six principal types of terrorist groups and correlates each type with an appropriate strategy of deterrent and remedial measures. The six types are defined according to two principal factors: (1) degree of commitment to political objectives (high, moderate, or low) and (2) utilization of criminal (i.e., robbery or "expropriation" to secure funds) tactics (criminal or noncriminal).[13]

Table 1   Six Principal Types of Terrorist Groups

Group Type	Degree of Commitment	Criminality
1	High	Noncriminal
2	High	Criminal
3	Moderate	Noncriminal
4	Moderate	Criminal
5	Low	Noncriminal
6	Low	Criminal

Each type displays a distinctive stance on the balance of risks that can be taken in pursuit of particular preferences. It is up to responsible government officials to adapt this decision-making taxonomy to proper and necessary counter-nuclear-terrorist efforts. These six types range from what might be termed "pure idealism" (Group Type 1) to what comes very close to being "pure criminality" (Group Type 6). Psychopathic or nihilistic terrorism may fall under the heading of either Group Type 5 or Group Type 6. (See Table 1 for the six principal types of terrorist groups. Table 2 gives the decision-making taxonomy based on these.)

Group Type 1

This type of terrorist group is characterized by a high degree of commitment to political objectives and an absence of criminal activity. Here, a self-sacrificing value system is in evidence, and the group does not secure needed funds through expropriatory activities. In view of the particular ordering of preferences associated with this type of terrorist group—an ordering that assigns much greater value to political objectives than to personal safety—deterrence efforts should focus upon threats to obstruct political objectives. Such threats must be directed at convincing the group that its resort to nuclear violence would mitigate against political objectives because it would both stiffen incumbent resolve and alienate vital bases of popular support. Deterrence might also be based upon a strategy of positive sanctions, in which certain rewards or concessions that relate to political objectives are promised in exchange for the nonuse of nuclear or higher-order weapons technologies. *Under no circumstances should deterrence of this type of terrorist group be based upon orthodox threats of physically punishing retaliation.*

Group Type 2

This type of terrorist group is characterized by a high degree of commitment to political objectives and by the utilization of criminal

Table 2   The Decision-Making Taxonomy

Group Type	Group Characteristics	Counternuclear Terrorist Strategy
1	High degree of political commitment; no criminal activity. Self-sacrificing value system. Preference ordering assigns far greater value to political objectives than to personal safety.	Deterrence focused upon threats to obstruct political objectives and promises to assist with such objectives in exchange for nonuse of nuclear weaponry. No threats of physically punishing retaliation.
2	High degree of political commitment; use of criminal tactics. Self-sacrificing value system. Preference ordering assigns far greater value to political objectives than to personal safety.	Deterrence focused upon same threats and promised concessions as in Group Type 1 *plus* efforts to exploit criminal character of the group. These efforts to concentrate upon creating a "bad press."
3	Moderate degree of political commitment; no criminal activity. No self-sacrificing value system. Preference ordering values both political objectives and personal safety.	Deterrence focused upon same threats and promises as in Group Type 1 *plus* an appropriate level of orthodox threats of physically punishing retaliation.
4	Moderate degree of political commitment; use of criminal tactics. Political concerns mirror Group Type 3.	Deterrence focused upon same threats and promises as in Group Type 3 *plus* efforts to publicize the group's ordinary criminal cast.
5	Low degree of political commitment; no criminal activity. Preference ordering values violence per se more highly than alleged political objectives. Group exhibits nihilistic/psychopathic traits.	Deterrence abandoned in favor of "prophylactic" preventive measures. Negative physical sanctions must be applied at highest reasonable levels. Waging of counternuclear terrorist campaign.
6	Low degree of political commitment; use of criminal tactics. Political concerns mirror Group Type 5. Group exhibits primary characteristics of bandit band; may also exhibit nihilistic/psychopathic traits as in Group Type 5.	Deterrence focused upon kinds of threats used against ordinary criminality *plus* preventive measures associated with Group Type 5.

Note: In all strategies involving positive sanctions, concessions should be based upon a predetermined (i.e., preincident) hierarchy of concessions rather than upon an ad hoc judgment of what can be allowed.

tactics. Here, the self-sacrificing value system is still in evidence, although the group secures needed funds through robberies of one kind or another. It follows that deterrence efforts should focus upon the same threats and promises associated with Group Type 1 *plus* efforts that publicize the criminal character of the group.

Group Type 3

This type of terrorist group is characterized by a moderate degree of commitment to political objectives and by an absence of criminal activity. Here, the group's primary rationale and concern is still manifestly political, but there is no evidence of the self-sacrificing values. And the group does not secure funds through expropriation. In view of the particular ordering of preferences associated with this type of terrorist group—an ordering that values both political objectives and personal safety—deterrence efforts should focus upon the same threats and promises associated with Group Type 1 *plus* an appropriate level of orthodox threats of physically punishing retaliation. Such negative sanctions are needed to compensate for the diminished (compared to Group Type 1 and Group Type 2) level of political commitment.

Group Type 4

This type of terrorist group is characterized by a moderate degree of commitment to political objectives and by the utilization of criminal tactics. Here, the group's political concerns mirror Group Type 3, but the group does secure funds through robberies and holdups. It follows that deterrence efforts should focus upon the same threats and promises associated with Group Type 3 *plus* efforts to publicize the group's ordinary criminal activities. As in the case of deterrence efforts associated with Group Type 2, such efforts are designed to alienate the group from vital bases of potential support.

Group Type 5

This type of terrorist group is characterized by a low degree of commitment to political objectives and by the absence of criminal activity. Here, the group's raison d'être is only nominally political, and the group does not secure funds through expropriation. Typically, this type of group looks upon violence as its own end rather than as an instrument. Moreover, violence is viewed as a romantic and creative force that is self-justifying. In view of the particular ordering of preferences associated with this type of terrorist group—an ordering that values the violent act itself more highly than any alleged political objectives—deterrence should be abandoned altogether as a strategy of counter–nuclear terrorism.

Because such groups exhibit traits that are best described an nihilistic or psychopathic, preventive measures should focus upon "prophylaxis" via a counter-nuclear-terrorism campaign that may or may not require preemption. And because personal safety figures unimportantly in this type of terrorist group's risk calculus, the application of negative physical sanctions must be at the highest reasonable levels—levels that are consistent with the society's basic commitment to decency and essential human rights.

Group Type 6

This type of terrorist group is characterized by a low degree of commitment to political objectives and by the use of criminal tactics. Here, the group's nominal political concerns mirror those of Group Type 5, but the group does secure funds through expropriation. Although this type of terrorist group may also exhibit nihilistic or psychopathic traits, its primary characteristics come closer to those of ordinary criminals or bandits. It follows that deterrence efforts should focus upon the kinds of threats that are used to counter orthodox criminality, and that these efforts must be augmented by the preventive measures associated with Group Type 5. The extent to which such preventive measures should be adopted depends largely on the extent to which this type of terrorist group exhibits nihilistic/psychopathic rather than purely criminal traits.

Behavioral Measures at the International Level

Counter-nuclear-terrorist strategies within states require differentiating sanctions according to the particular type of terrorist group involved. However, because nuclear terrorism might take place across national boundaries, the basic principles of these strategies must also be applied internationally. This means that those nations that are most vulnerable to nuclear terrorist attack must learn to call upon the doctor as well as the locksmith. Although it is critical for them to harden the target, it is also essential that they learn to soften the adversary. This means learning to understand the variety of terrorist-group preferences and the subtlety of ways in which these preferences may be exploited.

Of course, there are special difficulties involved in implementing behavioral measures of counter–nuclear terrorism internationally. These difficulties center on the fact that certain states sponsor and host terrorist groups and that such states extend the privileges of sovereignty to insurgents on their land. Although it is true that international law forbids a state to allow its territory to be used as a base for aggressive operations against another state with which it is not at war, a state that seeks to deal with terrorists hosted in another state is still in a very difficult position.

To cope with these difficulties, like-minded governments must create special patterns of international cooperation. These patterns must be based upon the idea that even sovereignty must yield to gross inversions of the norms expressed in the Charter of the United Nations; the Universal Declaration of Human Rights; the International Covenant on Economic, Social, and Cultural Rights; the International Covenant on Civil and Political Rights; the Convention on the Prevention and Punishment of the Crime of Genocide; the European Convention for the Protection of Human Rights and Fundamental Freedoms; the American Convention on Human Rights; the Nuremberg principles; and the 1949 Geneva Conventions. They must, therefore, take the form of collective defense arrangements between particular states that promise protection and support for responsible acts of counter–nuclear terrorism.

Such arrangements must entail plans for cooperative intelligence gathering on the subject of terrorism and for exchange of the information produced; an expanded and refined tapestry of agreements on extradition of terrorists; multilateral forces to infiltrate terrorist organizations and, if necessary, to take action against them;[14] concerted use of the media to publicize terrorist activities and intentions; and counterterrorism emergency medical networks. Such arrangements might also entail limited and particular acts directed toward effective counter–nuclear terrorism.

To implement these sorts of arrangements, states may need to enact appropriate forms of domestic law. In the United States, as part of the Comprehensive Crime Control Act (1984), Congress approved an Act for the Prevention and Punishment of the Crime of Hostage-Taking. Following the provisions of the Hostages Convention (1979), the act punishes the seizure or detaining of a person, coupled with threats to kill or injure the person or to continue to detain him or her, for the purpose of compelling a third person or a governmental organization to do or abstain from doing any act as an explicit or implicit condition for the release of the detained person.

To fully implement its responsibilities under the Convention for the Suppression of Unlawful Acts Against the Safety of Civil Aviation (Montreal Convention, 1973), the United States enacted the Aircraft Sabotage Act as part of the Comprehensive Crime Control Act of 1984. Moreover, to authorize the United States (specifically the attorney general and the secretary of state) to pay rewards of up to $500,000 for information concerning terrorist activity, Congress enacted the Act to Combat International Terrorism (1984). Taken together, these recent U.S. legislative measures contribute to the ability of the United States to cooperate internationally against terrorism.[15]

Other arrangements might center on encouraging dissension among the various terrorist groups. Such arrangements would seem to be especially promising if applied to the various factions of the Palestinian movement. Internecine struggles within this movement have been obvious since the mid-1970s, when Arafat's PLO (Palestine Liberation Organization) faction of Fatah, Al Saiqa, and PDFLP (Popular Democratic Front for the Liberation of Palestine) drew opposition from PFLP (Popular Front for the Liberation of Palestine), ALF (Arab Liberation Front), and PFLP-GC (Popular Front for the Liberation of Palestine–General Command) "rejectionists."

Above all else, however, international arrangements for counter-nuclear-terrorist cooperation must include sanctions for states that sponsor or support terrorist groups and activities.[16] As in the case of sanctions applied directly to terrorists, such sanctions may include carrots as well as sticks. Until every state in the world system calculates that support of counter-nuclear-terrorist measures is in its own interests, individual terrorist groups will have reason and opportunity to escalate their violent excursions.

Additional Measures Under International Law

The international legal order has tried to cope with transnational terrorism since 1937, when the League of Nations produced two conventions to deal with the problem. These conventions proscribed acts of terror-violence against public officials, criminalized the impairment of property and the infliction of general injuries by citizens of one state against those of another, and sought to create an international criminal court with jurisdiction over terrorist crimes. The advent of World War II, however, prevented the ratification of either document. An international criminal court[17] is, moreover, unlikely to come into being. But there are other measures under international law that could and should be used in the arsenal of international counter-nuclear-terrorism measures.

The principle of *aut dedere aut punire* ("extradite or prosecute") needs to be applied uniformly to terrorists. And the customary excepting of political offenses as reason for extradition must be abolished for acts of terrorism.[18] Although such practices would appear to impair the prospects of legitimate rights to self-determination and human rights, those proclaiming such rights should not be exempted from the prevailing norms of humanitarian law. At the moment, the ideological motives of the accused are given too much weight by certain states acting upon extradition requests. Although ideological motive should be considered as a mitigating factor in the imposition of punishment, it must not be regarded as the basis for automatic immunity.

To understand the consequences of overemphasizing political motives for refusing extradition in matters concerning terrorism, we need only consider the case of several self-styled U.S. black militants who hijacked a Delta DC-8 jet from Miami to Algiers in 1972. In 1975, a French court refused a U.S. request for their extradition because their admitted crime had been inspired by "political motives." In November 1978, the group received very light sentences, ranging from two and a half to three years, in a trial hailed by the defense as a "slap at American racism" and a "trial on American history." In short, the hijacking was judged a political crime because of what was characterized as "a pattern of institutionalized racism in the United States" involving "police brutality, job discrimination, school segregation, poverty and hunger."

An even more flagrant abuse of the political-offense grounds for refusing extradition took place in the same month as the French hijacking trial. In this case, Yugoslavia refused to extradite four West Germans wanted by Bonn on charges including the abduction and murder of industrialist Hanns-Martin Schleyer. Moreover, instead of prosecuting the alleged terrorists themselves, Yugoslavia declared the four persona non grata and allowed them to leave "to a country of their own choice." Speculation suggests that this country was Libya, Iraq, or South Yemen.

Under international law, the Yugoslavian action was improper for at least two reasons: (1) The political offense exception for refusing extradition must be waived in matters involving homicide; and (2) pursuant to longstanding customary norms and a number of recent conventions (the Tokyo Convention of 1963; the Hague Convention of 1971; the Montreal Convention of 1973; the Convention to Prevent and Punish Acts of Terrorism Taking the Form of Crimes Against Persons and Related Extortion That Are of International Significance of 1973; and the United Nations Convention on the Prevention and Punishment of Crimes Against Internationally Protected Persons of 1977), the extradite-or-prosecute formula applies.

A more recent case involves the October 7, 1985, seizure by Palestinian gunmen of the Italian cruise ship *Achille Lauro*. After taking custody of the hijackers, Egypt decided against prosecuting the gunmen *and* against extraditing them to another country with appropriate jurisdiction. Instead, it decided to surrender the terrorists to the custody of the PLO, a clear violation of international law because nonstate organizations lack legal personality. The subsequent U.S. interception of the Egyptian aircraft flying the hijackers to freedom—an interception that brought the gunmen before Italian courts—must be understood as a law-enforcing action. With its failure to abide by the extradite-or-prosecute formula, Egypt forfeited its ordinary immunity from interference in aviation.

Of course, the Yugoslavian and Egyptian actions illustrate a basic fact about the outlook for improved international legal steps regarding extradition of terrorists. This fact is simply that individual states base their extradition judgments primarily on narrow political grounds. It follows that strategies of counterterrorism should focus upon means to convince states that their own long-term interests can never be served by proterrorist extradition decisions. To fail to recognize these strategies is to commit the fallacy of legalism in the search for counterterrorist procedures. This does not mean, however, that the search for a fair, precise, and comprehensive set of guidelines concerning jurisdiction and extradition should be abandoned altogether. Quite the contrary! The identification of such a set of guidelines could assist states in harmonizing their own judgments of self-interest with explicit norms of international law.

States must creatively interpret the Definition of Aggression approved by the General Assembly in 1974. This definition condemns the use of "armed bands, groups, irregulars or mercenaries, which carry out acts of armed force against another State," but supports wars of national liberation against "colonial and racist regimes or other forms of alien domination." If it is interpreted too broadly, such a distinction[19] leaves international law with too little leverage in counter-nuclear-terrorist strategies. But if it is interpreted too narrowly, it places international law in the position of defending the status quo at all costs.

The problem, of course, is allowing international law to serve the interests of international order without impairing the legitimate objectives of international justice. But who is to determine the proper balance? Like all things human, force wears the Janus face of good and evil at the same time. It is an age-old problem, and one not adequately answered by identifying the institutional responsibility of the Security Council. The deliberate vagueness of the language of the Definition of Aggression is less of an obstacle than an opportunity if states can see their way clearly to sensible ad hoc judgments.

But how can they make judgments? What criteria can be applied to distinguish between legitimate claims for human rights and/or national liberation and illegitimate acts of terror? As we have seen, individual states must bear the ultimate responsibility for distinguishing between terrorists and freedom fighters. First, careful assessments must be made of insurgent conformance with the legal standard of "just cause." Second, states must assess *discrimination* and *proportionality* in the insurgent use of force.

In the words of the Report of the General Assembly's Ad Hoc Committee on International Terrorism in 1973: "Even when the use of force is legally and morally justified, there are some means, as in every form of human conflict, which must not be used; the legitimacy of a cause does not in itself legitimize the use of certain forms of violence, especially against the innocent." By itself, suffering cannot justify indiscriminacy and disproportionality in the use of force. As Elie Wiesel has argued, "Suffering confers neither privileges nor rights; it all depends on how one uses it. If you use it to increase the anguish of others, you are degrading, even betraying it."[20]

Perhaps the quintessence of the argument against suffering as justification for indiscriminacy and disproportionality was made by Elie Wiesel in the conclusion of his "Letter to a Young Palestinian Arab":

> I do feel responsible for what happened to you, but not for what you chose to do as a result of what happened to you. I feel responsible for your sorrow, but not for the way you use it, for in its name you have massacred innocent people, slaughtered children. From Munich to Maalot, from Lod to Entebbe, from hijacking to hijacking, from ambush to ambush, you have spread terror among unarmed civilians and thrown into mourning families already too often visited by death. You will tell me that all these acts have been the work of your extremist comrades, not yours; but they acted on your behalf, with your approval, since you did not raise your voice to reason with them. You will tell me that it is your tragedy which incited them to murder. By murdering, they debased that tragedy, they betrayed it. Suffering is often unjust, but it never justifies murder.[21]

For the United States, the chief danger of terrorism lies not in the guerrilla camps of Central America and southern Africa. That danger lies in ourselves. To meet the requirements of effective counterterrorism, the United States must oppose repressive regimes and movements whatever their ideological stripe. It must also support those insurgencies that spring from genuinely "just cause" and that are carried out with due regard for the laws of war of international law. The United States can't have it both ways. There is little point to U.S. condemnations of state-supported terrorism against U.S. interests in the Middle East if the United States supports its own terrorists in Central America.[22] Moreover, there is little point in bemoaning terrorist indifference to the humanitarian rules of armed conflict when contra rebels display total disregard for these rules.[23]

Recent attempts to counter terrorism by the Reagan administration reveal the importance of consistency in observing international law. In view of Egypt's failure to prosecute the Palestinian hijackers of the *Achille Lauro* or to extradite them to another country with appropriate jurisdiction,[24] the interception by U.S. Navy warplanes must be understood as a law-enforcing action. This is because the prerogatives of sovereignty are not absolute; they cannot be invoked to preempt punishment of a major crime committed against the nationals of another state.

Yet, the correct actions taken by the Reagan administration to oppose terrorism in the Middle East stand in ironic contrast to its proterrorist stance in Nicaragua. Refusing to submit to the compulsory jurisdiction of the World Court (International Court of Justice) in the case brought by Nicaragua, the administration can hardly lay claim to lawfulness. In this connection, U.S. credibility as a rule-abiding member of the community of nations is further undermined by the administration's direct violation of the World Court's final judgment of June 27, 1986, a judgment requiring the United States to refrain from any continued support of the contras.

By its forceful action against the Palestinian hijackers who defiled every civilized standard of humanitarian international law—hijackers who are characterized in law as "common enemies of mankind"—the Reagan administration advanced the highest principles of engagement in the war against terrorism. But in its relations with Nicaragua, the administration still casts its lot with the terrorists. Driven by ideological antipathy for a Marxist regime in this hemisphere, President Reagan has willfully subordinated the rule of law to the presumed imperatives of power politics. Left unchanged, our inconsistent policies toward terrorism will generate worldwide indifference to U.S. indignation and far-reaching constraints on U.S. power.

Consider what has happened in the aftermath of the *Achille Lauro*. Several governments involved—specifically Egypt, Italy, Yugoslavia, and South Yemen—knowingly ignored legal obligations. Preferring to rid themselves of one or more parties to the crime to incurring certain risks of terrorism or recrimination, they displayed contempt for centuries-old norms of jurisdiction and punishment. Although it is unlikely that these governments would have acted differently if the United States were itself more consistent in opposing terrorism, one thing is certain: Because of the Reagan administration's double standard on terrorism, these governments need have no fear of condemnation from Washington. Armed with an understanding of the uneven policies of the United States, they have a decisive propaganda advantage that may soon silence all U.S. appeals for justice. The final casualty of this development would be manifest in the shredded remnants of our world legal order.

In the end, we learn from Goethe, "we depend upon creatures of our own making." Understood in terms of the U.S. imperative to combat nuclear terrorism, Goethe's wisdom suggests a far-reaching U.S. disengagement from the self-defeating dynamics of anti-Sovietism. Without such disengagement, the United States will continue to support authoritarian regimes as a "necessary evil."

There is another reason why steps toward U.S.-Soviet reconciliation would reduce the threat of anti-U.S. terrorism. At a moment in history at which the Soviets seek far-reaching efforts at arms control and disarmament, such steps could encourage them to offer certain geopolitical concessions in exchange for greater security from nuclear war. An example of such concessions might well be diminished Soviet support for states that sustain terrorist groups (for example, Libya).

If, indeed, the Soviet Union were genuinely assimilable to the spirit of evil—a current article of faith in Washington—no reconciliation would be possible. Engaged not in secular political competition but in a Final Battle between the Sons of Light and the Sons of Darkness, the United States would perceive no alternative to its support of repressive anti-Soviet regimes. And it would perceive no alternative to constant struggle for geopolitical advantage, a judgment that would be reciprocated by the Soviet Union. As a result, we could expect an increasing incidence of terrorism against the United States, including possible nuclear terrorism.

But the prevailing U.S. view of the Soviet Union is a caricature. Fashioned in the ruins of thought, this caricature draws the United States farther and farther away from its own interests. There is still time for a change in direction, one based on the differentiation between secular political competition and theological conflict. In acknowledging this differentiation, the United States could begin to understand the imperatives of effective counterterrorism. Abandoning the sterile polarity that obscures its mental horizon, the United States could begin to take its first essential steps toward real safety from nuclear terrorist attack.

We must not abandon our interests. Nor should we expect the Soviet Union to abandon its interests. Rather, we must understand that basing every element of U.S. foreign policy on its probable effect on the USSR is contrary to U.S. needs. Once it is understood that U.S.-Soviet cooperation is in the security interests of both countries, and that the Soviets can share in this understanding, the way will be clear to move toward a genuinely self-serving U.S. foreign policy. Founded upon an end to the naive cynicism of an endless cold war, this policy would acknowledge the importance of human rights *everywhere*. Only then would we begin to find safety from the peril of nuclear terrorism. Each superpower seeks to enlarge its power and influence in world affairs. Yet, in the absence of expanded patterns of cooperation, both the United States and the USSR will become increasingly unable to meet the domestic requirements of social-economic well-being. And both will become increasingly vulnerable to nuclear war and nuclear terrorism.

But how, exactly, can cooperation get under way? For the United States, the answer lies in (1) an incremental disengagement from support of manifestly authoritarian regimes and a corresponding acknowledgment that insurgents combatting such regimes may have just cause and need not necessarily be Soviet surrogates; (2) a renunciation of the right to install future authoritarian regimes anywhere in the world and a corresponding acknowledgement that such regimes would not necessarily serve U.S. interests against the Soviet Union; (3) an end to our lawless support of insurgencies operating against Marxist regimes (the Reagan Doctrine) and a corresponding acknowledgment that such regimes are not necessarily enemies of the United States;[25] and (4) a rejection of any insurgency that is carried out against noncombatant populations.

For its part, the Soviet Union must offer (1) concrete expression of its public and doctrinal disdain of terrorism[26] by opposing (together with its client states of Bulgaria, East Germany, and North Korea) "adventurist" anti-U.S./anti-Israel groups in Europe and the Middle East and by acknowledging that such groups are not authentic movements for national liberation; (2) a rejection of any insurgency that is carried out against noncombatant populations; (3) and end to support of states in the Middle East that harbor and sustain anti-U.S./anti-Israel terrorists (e.g., Libya, Syria) and a corresponding acknowledgment that these states do nothing to advance the interests of self-determination; (4) an end to shipments of arms to Cuba and Nicaragua (a quid pro quo for U.S. renunciation of lawless insurgencies against those countries); and (5) an end to its lawless occupation of Afghanistan.

6

Redefining National Interests: Planetization and Freedom from Nuclear Terrorism

The effectiveness of international strategies of counter–nuclear terrorism will depend upon the tractability of proterrorist states. Real effectiveness, therefore, requires commitment by all states to unity and relatedness. To realize this commitment, all states will have to work toward the replacement of our fragile system of realpolitik with a new world politics of globalism.

Preventing nuclear terrorism must thus be seen as one part of an even larger strategy, one that is geared to the prevention of all forms of international violence.[1] It would be futile to try to tinker with the prospect of nucler terrorism without affecting the basic structure of modern world politics. This structure is integral to all possibilities of an atomic apocalypse, and its re-visioning and reformation is central to all possibilities for survival.

The capacity to prevent nuclear terrorism is inseparable from a new consciousness by our national leaders. Amidst the precarious crosscurrents of global power relations, states must undertake prodigious efforts to resist the lure of primacy, focusing instead on the emergence of a new sense of global obligation. And these efforts must be undertaken very soon. The great French Enlightenment philosopher, Jean Jacques Rousseau, once remarked: "The majority of nations, as well as of men, are tractable only in their youth; they become incorrigible as they grow old." Understood in terms of the imperative to change direction in the search for peace, this suggests that unless these nations achieve such a change before losing their "youth," the chances for later success may be lost forever.

What is required, then, is a nuclear regime that extends the principles of nuclear-war avoidance to the problem of nuclear terrorism. The centerpiece of this universal regime must be the cosmopolitan understanding that all states, like all people, form one essential body and one true community. Such an understanding, that a latent oneness lies buried beneath the manifold divisions of our fractionated world, need not be based on the mythical attractions of universal brotherhood and mutual concern. Instead, it must be based on the idea that individual states, however much they may "dislike" each other, are tied together in the struggle for survival.

To illustrate this principle, consider the following analogy: The states in world politics coexist in much the same fashion as a group of herdsmen who share a common pasture and who feel it necessary to increase their respective herds as best they can. Even though these herdsmen have determined that it is in the best interests of enlarging personal profits to continue to increase their own herds, they are mistaken. They are mistaken because they have failed to consider the *combined effect* of their calculations. This effect, of course, is an overgrazed pasture that brings them all to economic ruination.

In world politics, national leaders continue to act as if the security of their respective states is based upon a steady increase in armaments. Like the herdsmen, the failure of these leaders to understand the combined effect of such reasoning leads to the very opposite of the condition they seek. It is a familiar pattern. So familiar, in fact, that we might expect the patently obvious defects of political "realism" to be scrupulously avoided. But they are not.

Consider one more analogy: The states in world politics are prone to act in the fashion of an audience in a crowded movie theater after someone has yelled "Fire!" Confronted with a sudden emergency, each member of the audience calculates that the surest route to safety is a mad dash for the nearest exit, no matter what might happen to others who happen to get in the way. The combined effect of such calculations, of course, is apt to be catastrophic. At any rate, it is apt to be much more unfortunate than would have been the case if the people in the audience had sought safety through cooperation.

In the manner of the people in the movie audience, states continue to misunderstand that their only safe course is one in which the well-being and security of each is determined from the standpoint of what is best for the system as a whole. The path to security that is founded upon the presumed advantages of preeminence in armaments is destined to fail. *Si vis pacem, para pacem.* If you want peace, prepare for peace. In order to avert the overwhelmingly destructive global nuclear catastrophe that is rooted in the "realist" path, decisive steps must be taken to involve world leaders in a more promising definition of national interest.

The problem is aggravated by the transformation of realpolitik that has been taking place for more than 2,000 years. Although the competitive search for security in the international state of nature has always yielded war, this search was traditionally founded on the idea that there exists no practical alternative, that playing according to the rules of power politics is an operational necessity. Today, however, this idea has been replaced by the celebration of realpolitik as a virtue unto itself. Representing a departure from the traditional political realism of Thucydides, Thrasymachus, and Machiavelli, this glorification of the state qua force flows from modifications in modern Europe, especially Germany. From Fichte and Hegel, through Ranke and Von Treitschke, these modifications have transformed the alleged facts of international statecraft into values. And although we may not accept Hegel's identification of the state as "the march of God in the world," we no longer seem to really contest its role as a stand-in for the deity.

The time has come for states to struggle as if with the painful movements of a lungfish, forcing old fins to become new legs. For those that lock their definitions of national interest into the dying forms of realpolitik, there can be only disaster. Faced with the awareness that the wave length of change is now shorter than the life span of a human being, states must replace the intransigence of nationalisms with faith in a new kind of power. This is the primordial power of unity and interdependence, an ecumenical power that can replace the centrifugal forces that have atomized nations with a fresh vision of *realism.*

To achieve this faith, states must be surrounded by a new field of consciousness—one that flows from a common concern for the human species and from the undimmed communion of individual nations with the entire system of nations. Living at an interface between world order and global disintegration, states must slough off the shackles of outmoded forms of self-interest. With the explosion of the myth of "realism," the global society of states could begin to come together in a renewed understanding of the connection between survival and relatedness. When this happens, states will finally consummate their search for planetization.

The task, then, is to make the separate states conscious of their emerging planetary identity. With such a re-visioning of national goals and incentives, states can progress to an awareness of new archetypes for global society. Because all things contain their own contradiction, the world system based upon militaristic nationalism can be transformed into an organic world society.

To succeed in this task will be very difficult. But it need not be as fanciful as some would have us believe. Indeed, before we take the shroud measurements of the corpse of human society, we must understand that faith in the new forms of international interaction is a critical step toward their implementation. Already, there is evidence that such faith is justified. We are, as philosopher William Irwin Thompson has suggested, at the "edge of history." It is a time to reaffirm that the truest forms of realism lie in the imaginings of idealists. In the words of Thompson:

> In the history of ideas a new idea is often first picked up by a crazy person, then elaborated by an artist who is more interested in its imaginative possibilities than in its literal truth; then it is picked up by a scholar or scientist who has become familiar with the idea through the work of the artist; the savant makes the hitherto crazy idea perfectly acceptable to the multitude, until finally the idea rests as a certainty in the hands of a bureaucracy of pedants.[2]

Thompson's use of the term "crazy person" is, of course, laced with irony. In a world wherein "sane" foreign policy is still tied to the preposterous lies of a "peace through strength" ideology, "sanity" can lead only to oblivion. In such a world, only a "crazy person" can harbor the kind of consciousness that is needed for survival. Time, as St. Augustine wrote, is more than the present as we experience it and the past as a present memory. It is also the future as a present expectation, and this expectation carries within itself the seeds of its own verification.

To fulfill the expectations of a new global society, one based on a more advanced stage of world evolutionary development, appropriate initiatives must be taken *within* states. Here is the primary arena of world order reform. National leaders can never be expected to initiate the essential changes on their own. Rather, the new evolutionary vanguard must grow out of informed publics throughout the world. Such a vanguard, aiming to end the separation and competition of states that is founded upon egoistic definitions of national interest, has been described by Dr. Jonas Salk.

> A new body of conscious individuals exists, expressing its desire for a better life for Man as a species and as individuals, eager to devote themselves to this end. Such groups, when they are able to coalesce through an understanding of their relatedness to one another and to the natural processes involved in "Nature's game" of survival and evolution, will find a strength and courage in sensing themselves as part of the Cosmos and as being involved in a game that is in accord with Nature and not anti-natural. These groups will initiate movements which, in turn, will be manifest in their effects not only upon the species and the planet but upon individual lives. Their benefit is likely to be expressed in a greater frequency, or proportion, of individuals finding increasing satisfaction and fulfillment in life.[3]

The vanguard that can change the destiny of the human race would act on the central understanding of Freud's great work *Civilization and*

Its Discontents. Just as any civilization requires a renunciation of certain private instincts, so does an organic world society require a renunciation of certain "instincts" of states. Just as civilized human beings have exchanged a portion of their possibilities of happiness for security, so must nations exchange a portion of their "egoistic" preferences for a chance at survival. Like individual peoples of the distant past, modern states must learn to understand that their primal period of "everyone for himself" cannot endure for very long.

Freud tells us that the replacement of the power of the individual person by the power of the entire community constitutes the decisive act of civilization. Building upon this insight, we may say that the replacement of the power of the individual state by the power of the entire global community constitutes the decisive step of *planetization.* This power of the entire global community is not coercive military power, but the power of a universalized and new consciousness, a clear vision of reality that substitutes wholeness and convergence for the fatal instincts of narcissism. In a struggle that Freud describes as a conflict between Eros and Death, between the instinct of life and the instinct of destruction, states must enter into the service of Eros, satisfying their vital needs in a spirit that recognizes the interrelatedness of their fates.

The United States Outside the World

The United States is microcosm. Its errors of realpolitik reveal and reinforce the errors of an entire world. Its rejection of genuine communion with other states makes worldwide communion impossible.

Where have we gone wrong? The answer has several components. We have confused violence with power. We have abandoned our interests and our ideals at the same time. We have substituted rhetoric for thought. And above all else, we have subordinated every principle and goal to the sterile dualism of U.S.-Soviet rivalry.

Our enemy is the Soviet Union. The Soviet Union is *always* our enemy. This is an Orwellian axiom of U.S. foreign policy behavior. It remains beyond question. To subject it to scrutiny is inexcusable. It is blasphemy.

Yet, if the Soviet Union did not exist, our leaders would have to invent it. Otherwise, to whom would we feel superior? To whom would we impute our frustrations, our weaknesses, our failures?

Our enemy in world politics must always be concrete. It cannot be vague and shifting, so ephemeral that there is no passionate focal point of hostility. Indeed, this enemy must be opposed passionately, as it is on the plane of passion that anti-Sovietism draws its only meaning.

It is also on the plane of passion that we may renounce any expectation from the Soviet Union of a course of conduct that is reasonable and self-interested. Everything is made clear and straightforward if we discern in the Kremlin a metaphysical principle that drives it to do evil under all circumstances. The Soviet Union, we are told, is *obliged* to do evil, not good; it cannot be reformed.

With this view, U.S. policy reveals its own insubstantiality. Allegedly the only pragmatic approach to world affairs, it is in fact unremittingly utopian. If the Soviet union is assimilable to the spirit of evil, no reconciliation or comparison is possible. Its will is one that commits itself purely, gratuitously to do harm. Thus, all global misfortune—crises, wars, famines, revolutions—take place because of Soviet interference.

U.S. supporters of this caricatural view are fearful of discovering that the world is ill-contrived, that there exist many causes of its problems, for then they would be compelled to understand a complicated reality. Rather than be burdened with an agonizing responsibility, they localize every hazard in the Soviet Union. Left unimpeded, however, such Manicheanism will have a self-fulfilling effect, creating the conditions under which one or the other superpower (or both) must be annihilated.

At its heart, the problem is one of individuals. Our leaders can exploit an anti-Soviet worldview only because it satisfies the particular cravings of people. This worldview brings special pleasures. By treating the Soviet Union as a pernicious society, Americans affirm at the same time that *they* belong to an elite, one that is based on goodness. There are no special requirements for membership in this elite, no standards of excellence that need to be met, only citizenship in the United States.

We begin to understand the human roots of current policy. Individual Americans support a protracted enmity with the Soviet Union largely out of fear of being alone. To this end, they find the existence of the Soviet adversary absolutely necessary. Small matter that the Soviet Union is essentially a state like their own, comprised of people like themselves. Because they have chosen to devalue reason at the outset, they are impervious to logic, responding only to the strong emotional benefits of the herd.

The Americans who embrace current policy may readily confess that their Soviet counterparts share a basic humanity. But this concession costs them nothing, for they have put this quality in parentheses. What matters is that a condition of sustained international enmity overcomes solitariness and mediocrity, that it enables membership in the crowd. These Americans have chosen to accept anti-Sovietism as an article of faith because that is something one cannot believe alone.

It follows from all this that before the United States can extricate itself from the predatory embrace of realpolitik, individual Americans will need to discover alternative and more authentic sources of reassurance. To a certain extent this process is already under way, animated by the manifestly contrived dualism offered by our leaders. Yet, the benefits of this process will accrue only to those people who display a measure of political awareness; they will be lost upon many millions of others who are unmoved by reason.

What is to be done about *these* people, those for whom the *angst* of our time is only the newest form of hubris? Although their politics is a lie, confirming a total disjunction between problem and solution, it is a politics that confers far-reaching ego satisfaction and self-esteem. Where are there appropriate substitute forms of such satisfaction?

To answer these questions we must first understand that the journey from the herd to personhood begins by myth and ends in doubt. For this journey to succeed, the individual traveling along the route must learn to substitute a system of uncertainties for what he or she has always believed; to learn to tolerate and encourage doubt as a replacement for the comforting woes of statism. Induced to live against the grain of our civilization, such individuals must become not only conscious of their singularity, but satisfied with it. Organically separated from civilization, they must become aware of the forces that undermine it, forces that offer them a last remaining chance for both meaning and survival.

We may turn to Kierkegaard for guidance. In *Point of View,* "That Individual," recognizing the "crowd" as "untruth," he warned of the dangers that lurk in submission to multitudes: "A crowd in its very concept is the untruth, by reason of the fact that it renders the individual completely impenitent and irresponsible, or at least weakens his sense of responsibility by reducing it to a fraction. . . . For "crowd" is an abstraction and has no hands: but each individual has ordinarily two hands. . . ." And what is the most degrading crowd of all? The answer was supplied not by Kierkegaard, but by Nietzsche in his *Zarathustra.* "State is the name of the coldest of all cold monsters. . . . The state tells lies in all the tongues of good and evil; and whatever it says it lies—and whatever it has it has stolen. Everything about it is false. . . . All-to-many are born: for the superfluous the state was invented."[4]

The task, then, is for each American to *become* an individual. Rejecting the idolatry of militaristic nationalism, each man and woman must understand the lethal encroachments of the state. Recognizing in the current leadership an incapacity to surmount collective misfortune (Nietzsche reminded us that "often mud sits on the throne—and often also the throne on mud"), each citizen must strive to produce his or her own private expression of progress. "From becoming an individual no one," said Kierkegaard, "is excluded, except he who excludes himself by becoming a crowd."

Worn threadbare, anti-Sovietism must cease to be our principal source of national meaning. Its replacement, however, must be authentic. To close what Pierre Teilhard de Chardin called, in *The Phenomenon of Man,* "the spherical thinking circuit," the American prisoner of realpolitik must learn to discover personal value in his own accomplishments, in his own private characteristics and contributions. Whatever bestows value and self-esteem, so long as it is not hurtful to others or beholden to nationality, advances the conditions of reason and an improved world order.

But such transformations cannot take place in a vacuum. Rather, they must be shaped by a sympathetic society, a network of values and orientations that would encourage and nurture personal growth. At the moment, such a network does not exist. Imprisoned by a materialism that overrides all other goals, Americans now stand in the ruins of consciousness. Melding back into the preformed mainstream of popular culture, we are wary of stepping out of line, careful to cultivate the trappings (but rarely the substance) of "success."

There is nothing new about such an indictment of American life. What is new—and what is deplorable—is that societal indifference to real personal growth has now become celebrated. Content to be casualties of a many-stranded system of manipulation, Americans have learned to *despise* individualism.

Intimate with falsehoods, we no longer expect truth. Languishing in the degradations of political hucksterism, we are exultant with banality and grateful for passivity. Everything is acceptable as long as it poses no threat to place and to order. The only enemy is change and decomposition.

None of this is to suggest that our foreign policy is "caused" by behavioral and social deficiencies, but only that such deficiencies are exploited for political effect. Were the world organized differently, in a fashion without multiple sovereignties and zero-sum perceptions, individual American needs would seek different sources of satisfaction. But we do live in a fragmented world of separate states, and in this world anti-Sovietism is made dominant by an ideology that feeds upon the weakness of individual persons. There is nothing about the present structure of international relations that makes anti-Sovietism inevitable; it comes about only because this structure combines with behavioral conditions in a way that transforms them both.

In Ionesco's play *The Lesson,* an aged teacher gives private instruction to an eager but obtuse female pupil. As the action proceeds, the teacher derives a progressive increase of power from his very role as *giver*, as one who prescribes meanings. However arbitrary or nonsensical his meanings, the words have only the significance *he* decides to bestow upon them. Any other meanings are "wrong."

A similar relationship exists between Americans and their political leaders. Dominated by theatrical manipulations of language, we remain sealed off from knowledge, cooperating in a process that will destroy us. In the fashion of the pupil whose subordination drains her vitality and ends in her rape and murder, we too are all too willing to yield. This is because we have allowed our "teachers" to profane knowledge to a point at which resistance seems out of place; indeed, at which dissent from official meanings is subversive.

We accept myth as meaning, the demands of an incessant anti-Sovietism as virtue. This is not the cause of our shallow society, a society that retards personhood and national security, but one of its results. Plato argued that our hopes for purposeful reconstruction of social life turn on an intolerance of myth in politics, but today it is the other way around. It is our infatuation with a deformed society that makes myth possible.

Myth, in this case, brings death. The danger is exacerbated by the accompanying illusion of our collective immortality. Refusing to believe in the possibility of our extinction as a nation, we recognize no compelling incentives for international coexistence. Even the nearness of a planetwide nuclear winter does nothing to waken us to truth. "Do not try to explain death to me," says Achilles to Odysseus in Hades. "Do not suggest that America can die," command the people of the United States as they stand face to face with the cessation of all life.

The illusions are connected. The incapacity to recognize our collective mortality is little more than an extension of each individuals' unwillingness to contemplate personal death. The remedy? It is, in Unamuno's words, from *The Tragic Sense of Life,* "to consider our mortal destiny without flinching, to fasten our gaze upon the gaze of the Sphinx, for it is thus that the malevolence of its spell is discharmed." Spinoza taught that freedom comes from a cultivated disregard for death, but such freedom is actually servitude. To consider that we must die—and that the aftermath of death is unknowable—is the starting point of understanding, of what Unamuno calls "the very palpitation of my consciousness."

If all of this sounds grandly unpolitical, it is because politics as usual cannot prevent nuclear terrorism. And if it all sounds hopelessly idealistic, it must be realized that nothing can be more fanciful than continuing on the present course. To be sure, today's idealists in foreign affairs—those who would seek to leave militaristically nationalistic states behind, whimpering in the corners of their egos—have little cause for optimism. Their search to actualize new forms of international interaction is unlikely to succeed. But it is the only search worth conducting. It is, therefore, the only approach worthy of the term *realism.*

But how, exactly, are we to begin this search? What can actually be done to bring about new forms of world politics? How can states reroute their narrowly self-interested modes of foreign policy activity to a more promising global orientation? How can national leaders begin to build upon the understanding that it is in their country's own best interests to develop strategies of international interaction from a systemic vantage point?

The answer, perhaps, lies in a self-conscious attempt to create an alternative configuration of world politics in which every state can identify the support of its own major preferences. As anyone may well imagine, this is no mean task. Indeed, there is an almost irresistible temptation to say with Schopenhauer, Spengler, and Tolstoy that any such attempt at global restructuring is the height of presumptuous nonsense. Can even the most gifted segments of humanity introduce an internationally selected and orderly movement into the *pluriversum* of modern world politics?

Clearly, in view of the heterogeneity of national value systems at work, this kind of configuration cannot reasonably expect to measure up to each state's optimal design, but it can still be *acceptable* to all of them. Scholars and statesmen can begin an expansive exploration of alternative world futures in an attempt to identify an appropriate "mix." Such exploration would be essential as planetization must rest upon a broad variety of compromises between states.

Dimensions for the Design
of Alternative World Futures

There are three principal dimensions that might be used to characterize and design an improved system of world order. These dimensions are structure, process, and context. By exploring a variety of global alternatives along each of these dimensions, statesmen and scholars can begin the urgently needed program of national and planetary restructuring that is a sine qua non for freedom from nuclear terrorism.

Structure

A number of ways exist of casting models of world order in terms of structure, that is, the prevailing distribution of global power. Typically, these ways center on the distinction between bipolar and multipolar world systems.[5] There are, however, a number of more complex structural conceptualizations that might be considered. In exploring the planetization implications of such pattern-images, national decisionmakers and scholars may systematically address themselves to planetary design according to structure.

There is no historical evidence that tends to support the contention that the only time in history of the world that we have had any extended periods of peace is when there has been a balance of power.[6] And there is no persuasive logical argument that points to the general conclusion that it is when one nation becomes more powerful in relation to its potential competitor that the danger of war arises.[7] Indeed, the first of these statements is entirely inaccurate whereas the second ignores some of the most serious dangers that inhere in today's nuclear system. From the standpoint of history, periods of balance have inevitably yielded periods of war. From the standpoint of logic, perceptions of balance in power relations need have no effect on the likelihood of warfare, whatever its form and whatever the nature of its participants.[8]

There is also no reason to believe that even a truly symmetrical balance (which neither the United States nor the Soviet Union would ever encourage) would prevent hegemony. This is because it is erroneous that all of the major powers share a *preeminent* concern for preventing disproportionalities of power that lead to dominance, and that each major actor will act accordingly. The assumption that states always rank the prevention of hegemony at the apex of their particular preference orderings is erroneous because it suggests that such prevention is always believed by each state to be in its own best interests. In fact, there is certainly *no* reason to believe that states will consistently value the avoidance of hegemony more highly that alternative preferences. Any of the leading state actors in a symmetrical multipower balance system may, on occasion, calculate that the benefits that are expected to accrue from hegemony by any one state are great enough to warrant the probable costs.

But there is really no reason to dwell on the antihegemony implications of a symmetrical balance situation because such a situation is remarkably implausible. The principal members of the favored balance arrangement are patently asymmetrical. The United States and the Soviet Union are not well matched along the economic dimension, whereas Japan and Western Europe are military peers of neither superpower. And China's developing military power is still unparalleled on the economic front. It follows that a realistic analysis of the multipolar system must take as its starting point the idea of an asymmetrical balance—an idea that may very well be a glaring contradiction in terms.

A third reason for doubting that current multipolarism will be capable of preventing hegemony centers on the absence of a "swing" state, or "balancer." Ironically, this feature of the new balance system touted as "proof" of departure from classical balance dynamics is actually a drawback from the standpoint of thwarting heady ideas by major powers. This is because a major power strongly committed to the balancer role and perceived as such by every other major power might magnify the anticipated costs of hegemony to the point where such costs would exceed prospective gains. Assuming that national decision makers choose rationally between alternative courses of action, this means that perceptions of a powerful and committed balancer might signal a crucial or even necessary input into the decisional calculi of states contemplating hegemony.

The multipolar balance system also contains an inherent contradiction between its commitment to more durable and strengthened alliances and its encouragement of multipolar tendencies. In effect, these are competing values. Alliance reliability is apt to be greater in bipolar world systems than in multipolar ones. The trend back toward the flexible alignments of the classical balance system that is signaled by the loosening of hierarchic ties within a major coalition represents a trend back toward mercurial forms of collaboration. This is because the reliability of alliances is apt to vary inversely with the number of systemwide axes of conflict.

The worthiness of multipolarism is also undercut by its essential reliance upon diplomacy and by its increased measure of decisional uncertainty. As a result of the expanded number of major actors and probable axes of conflict, would-be aggressor states would find it increasingly difficult to anticipate the retaliatory consequences of their actions. Such difficulty concerns the probable source as well as the substance of reciprocity. Although this increased measure of uncertainty might inhibit the willingness to aggress in certain instances, it very likely provides a less effective deterrent than that offered by the high probability of punishment associated with bipolar systems.

The increased uncertainty that characterizes multipolar world systems also creates specific disadvantages for counterterrorism. These disadvantages may manifest themselves via the activity of terrorist actors, or through the activities of their host states. In the first case, terrorists are able to parlay this uncertainty into greater freedom of action for themselves. This is because prospective state targets of terrorist actors would be apt to find it more difficult to rely upon alliance partners for support of antiterrorist measures in a multipolar world system. In the second case, host states whose foreign policies and power relations are affected by their terrorist guests may take aggressive steps toward other states more readily than they would in the less uncertain bipolar world.

This discussion points to the conclusion that the essential logic of peaceful global relations in a decentralized world system is subverted by the operational dynamics of multipolarism. What all of this suggests, of course, is not the need to abandon multipolar conceptions in the search for an improved structural model of world order (at a minimum, the requirements of feasibility compel leaders and scholars to continue the search within a basic framework of multipolarism), but rather the need to improve the methodological underpinnings of this search. The adequacy of any structural alternative to the present system of world order is necessarily contingent upon the quality of the scholarship that leads to its formulation. In addressing themselves to planetary design according to structure, leaders and scholars must subject their tentative preferences to the scrutiny of sound logical analysis. Only then can they be in a position to determine gaps between alleged virtues and actual promise.

In order to narrow the gap between model and reality, students of counter–nuclear terrorism needn't abandon their basic conceptualizations altogether. All they must do is subdivide those conceptualizations with the introduction of an important intervening variable: the power of terrorist actors. As an example, the scholar who wishes to preserve a bipolar characterization of world politics can simply create a variety of appropriate subcategories based upon terrorist power.

The actual number of these categories will depend upon the precise manner in which the intervening variable is described (for example, if it is treated dichotomously—large extent, small extent—there will be two subcategories; if it is treated trichotomously—large extent, moderate extent, small extent—there will be three subcategories, etc.). Of course, this manner of subdivision may be applied to multipolar, multibloc, or any other basic structural models as well. In this way, scholars may reconcile their principal characterizations of structure with the increasing influence of terrorist actors.

The most basic way in which terrorist power may be introduced into existing structural models is simply to note whether or not such power exists at all. This means introducing a dichotomous distinction between terrorist actors sharing in the power and such actors not sharing in the power. If the underlying world system structure is described as bipolar, a ready-made set of models becomes available. Figure 1 describes the conceptions of Wolfram Hanrieder.[9]

Professor Hanrieder subdivides the bipolar universe of cases according to (1) the ratio of power between blocs, and (2) whether or not secondary actors share in the power. The two kinds of bipolarity treated (symmetrical—equal ratio of power between blocs; asymmetrical—unequal ratio of power between blocs) become "hetero" systems whenever sec-

Figure 1 Models of Bipolar World System Structure

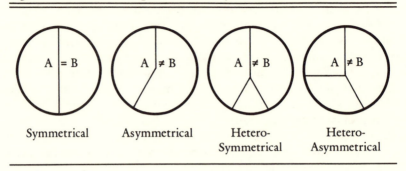

| Symmetrical | Asymmetrical | Hetero-Symmetrical | Hetero-Asymmetrical |

ondary actors enter into the picture. These secondary actors, however, refer to *states*. Nowhere do they extend to terrorist actors.

But this does not prevent us from translating the Hanrieder models to suit our own purposes. Indeed, when we tie our definition of secondary actors to terrorist actors, these models provide exactly what is needed. Here, "hetero" systems become those forms of bipolarity in which certain distinct kinds of *nonstate actors* share in the power.

These models immediately reveal an important pattern of interdependence in bipolar systems. This pattern concerns the relationship between the ratio of power between blocs and the extent of terrorist power. Not only does the ratio of power between blocs seriously affect the extent of terrorist power, but this extent in turn affects the ratio of power between blocs.

This kind of ongoing interaction may have serious implications for the student of counter–nuclear terrorism. The point of the redefined heterosymmetrical and heteroasymmetrical models is twofold: (1) They may *alert* the scholar to the relationship in the first place; or (2) they may allow for accurate conceptualization once the relationship has been detected in some other manner, that is, after a number of historical materials have been scrutinized. Just which purpose the models will serve in any given case depends upon the individual scholar's particular strategy of inquiry (whether he or she prefers to begin by scrutinizing abstract models or empirical cases.)

One way in which terrorist actors may affect the ratio of power between blocs is by exerting influence on their host states. Terrorist actors may have a particularly important effect on their host states' collective defense arrangements. Depending upon the relationship between these actors and their state hosts, the alliance position of the latter may vary considerably. More exactly, where this is the kind of relationship in which the host state is in full control of terrorist activities, there exists no special reason to doubt the credibility of its alliance commitments. On the other hand, where the state actor is clearly an unwilling host and not in complete control of terrorist activities, its prospective ability to honor alliance commitments may be seriously undermined. The cumulative effects of this kind of relationship between host states and terrorist actors may, in turn, seriously affect the ratio of power between blocs.

In exploring the ways in which terrorist actors influence the ratio of power between blocs, we may also assess their effects on alliances generally. For one thing, the pressure of terrorist actors may affect the *number* of alignments between states. It may occasion additional alliances among states that are commonly opposed to terrorist activities, inhibit prospective alliances in which split sympathies are in evidence, or even break up existing alignments that are crosscut by this kind of split. In certain instances, this sort of breakup might result in new and different alignments and perhaps even an entirely new global structure. If the original structure were a "tight" bipolar one, it might be transmuted into some form of "loose" bipolarity. If it were loose bipolar to begin with, it might be transformed into a multipolar system.

The ratio of power between blocs may also affect the extent of terrorist power. Just *how* it affects this depends largely on (1) whether the blocs are split in their sympathies to terrorist actors, and (2) the extent to which the ratio of power between blocs is paralleled by this split. For example, if the blocs were split in their feelings about terrorist actors along bloc lines and the more powerful bloc were sympathetic, these actors could expect a far more satisfactory context for their efforts than they would if the situation were reversed. Their operating milieu would be less propitious were the more powerful bloc the unsympathetic one. In those cases in which feelings toward terrorist actors are *not* divided along bloc lines, there is no reason to believe that the ratio of power between blocs is particularly important to terrorist power.

More complex conceptualizations of multipolarity. To this point, we have considered ways in which terrorist power may be introduced into bipolar models as an intervening variable. More exactly, we have shown that the Hanrieder models may be redefined such that "hetero" systems become those forms of bipolarity in which terrorist actors (rather than state actors) share in the power. Although no ready-made models exist for multipolar world systems in this sense, there is no reason to believe that they are intrinsically less susceptible to subdivision.

Scholars who wish to characterize the basic system structure as multipolar while taking terrorist actors into account may begin with the simple distinction between (1) multipolar power systems in which terrorist actors do not share in the power and (2) multipolar power systems in which terrorist actors do share in the power. Thereafter, the second class of cases may be subdivided according to the prevailing ratio of power between national actors (rather than blocs, as in the bipolar case). This ratio may have important implications for terrorist power. Alternatively, terrorist power may have decisive consequences for the ratio of power between national actors.

For example, terrorist power may affect the ratio of power between national actors in much the same way as it affects the ratio of power between blocs in a bipolar system. These means include the exertion of pressure on host states and the instigation or breakup of various kinds of interstate alignments. Terrorist power may also affect the ratio of power between national actors in other ways. One way concerns the formation of "heterogeneous" alignments, that is, alignments between states and terrorist actors. Such collaboration may strengthen the state partners by offering them a means of acting through their nonstate allies. As we know, this new opportunity for acting with impunity may greatly increase the likelihood of international aggression.

Another way in which terrorist power may affect the ratio of power between national actors concerns the formation of alliances in which both parties are terrorist actors. To an increasing extent, terrorist organizations are claiming de jure status for themselves, negotiating agreements with each other in the process. The cumulative effects of these counterstate alignments may be profoundly important. In the most obvious sense, they may contribute to the overthrow of established governments or established policies. The ratio of power between national actors may also affect the extent of terrorist power in multipolar systems. As in the case of bipolar systems, in which the appropriate ratio is between blocs, the importance of the ratio of power between national actors depends largely on the prevailing pattern of sympathies toward terrorist actors and on the extent to which this pattern is paralleled by differences in power.

When national actors are split in their feelings toward terrorist actors, the power of the latter will depend to a significant extent upon the ratio of power between the sympathetic and unsympathetic states. Terrorist power will be enhanced to the extent that sympathetic states are more powerful and diminished to the extent that unsympathetic states have the upper hand. If, however, the power of sympathetic and unsympathetic states were roughly equal, the ratio of power between national actors would be unimportant to terrorist power. Similarly, if national actors were not split in their feelings toward terrorist actors, the ratio of power between the former would be of no particular importance to terrorist power. Such a condition might exist if virtually all state actors were of one opinion on this question, irrespective of what that particular opinion might be.

This information about the bases of terrorist power can now be used to create more useful structural conceptualizations of the world system. To this point, our discussion of both bipolar and multipolar systems has simply centered upon terrorist actors sharing in the power. No formal use has yet been made of the particular extent of sharing involved. Using the information from the above discussion, however, both bipolar and multipolar systems in which terrorist actors share in the power may now be subdivided further according to the degree of sharing in evidence.

Bipolarity. Our earlier discussion of bipolarity centered on two basic models. Each of these models was characterized by the presence of terrorist actors. The difference between them concerned the ratio of power between blocs. This ratio was equal in the heterosymmetrical system and unequal in the heteroasymmetrical one.

With the introduction of the extent of terrorist power as an intervening variable, each of these basic universes of cases may be broken down further. Exactly how many subcases may be created from the heterosymmetrical and heteroasymmetrical systems will depend upon the way the intervening variable is treated. If it is treated dichotomously (for example, large extent, small extent), there will be four basic patterns rather than two:

Heterosymmetrical	Heteroasymmetrical
a. large extent	a. large extent
b. small extent	b. small extent

If it is treated trichotomously (for example, large extent, moderate extent, small extent), there will be six basic patterns, and so on. The advantage of this kind of subdivision is that is facilitates accurate structural modeling of world politics. At the same time, care must be taken to avoid the construction of too many "boxes." Any model is necessarily a simplification, and although accurate representation is a primary objective, it must not be accomplished at the expense of generality. It follows that anything more complex than trichotomous treatment of our intervening variable is likely to yield too large a number of structural models.

Multipolarity. In our discussion of multipolarity, we had no ready-made set of models at hand. Unlike the bipolar case, therefore, we spoke of no particular number of basic configurations. Rather, we implied that there could be as many multipolar models with terrorist actors under investigation as there were ways of characterizing the ratio of power between national actors. If this intervening variable were treated dichotomously (for example, equal, unequal), there would be two basic models.

If equality and inequality might coexist at different levels of the system (for example, the presence of a major power–minor power distinction signifies a condition of inequality between classes of actors that might be paralleled by equality within one or both classes), a trichotomous treatment of the intervening variable would become possible. Here, we would speak of an equal ratio, an unequal ratio, and a "mixed" or equal-unequal ratio. In this case there would be three basic models of multipolar world systems.

With the extent of terrorist power as a second intervening variable, each of these basic multipolar models or universes of cases may be subdivided further. Once again, exactly how many additional cases may be created depends upon the particular manner in which the extent of terrorist power is handled. If we start with the two basic multipolar systems mentioned above, and treat the second intervening variable dichotomously, we will have four new universes of cases:

Equal Ratio	Unequal Ratio
a. large extent	a. large extent
b. small extent	b. small extent

If we start with the two basic multipolar systems, and treat extent of terrorist power trichotomously, we will construct six new universes of cases:

Equal Ratio	Unequal Ratio
a. large extent	a. large extent
b. moderate extent	b. moderate extent
c. small extent	c. small extent

If we start out with the three basic multipolar systems mentioned, and treat the second intervening variable dichotomously, we will also have six new universes of cases. But these, of course, will be somewhat different from the earlier set of six (two will be new, and two that were present in the first set of six will be absent in the second):

Equal Ratio	Mixed Ratio	Unequal Ratio
a. large extent	a. large extent	a. large extent
b. small extent	b. small extent	b. small extent

Finally, if we start with the three basic multipolar systems and treat the extent of terrorist power trichotomously as well, we will create nine new universes of cases:

Equal Ratio	Mixed Ratio	Unequal Ratio
a. large extent	a. large extent	a. large extent
b. moderate extent	b. moderate extent	b. moderate extent
c. small extent	c. small extent	c. small extent

What we have created here are several new structural models of world politics. By taking into account the power of terrorist actors as well as of states, these models provide much more accurate renderings of global structure than their more basic "parent" ones. At the same time, they are not yet "too complex." Their creation is informed by the introduction of a limited number of intervening variables into the basic bipolar and multipolar models. Any one of these new models may now be investigated from the standpoint of planetization and freedom from nuclear terrorism.

Hypotheses and Models. But these models must not be investigated at random. The choice of models of investigation must be determined by a particular problem in question and by suggested explanations for that problem. In short, inquiry must begin with specific hypotheses, and models must be selected accordingly. The models provide the context within which hypotheses may be explored. To investigate the models without the benefit of particular hypotheses is to put the cart before the horse. In such cases, there exists no criterion by which to determine what facts are relevant to the exploration of the model. Here, "explanation" is backward.

For example, if we were interested in discovering the effects of terrorist presence on power management (war avoidance) in bipolar systems, we might advance an appropriate hypothesis. To begin to explore the hypothesis we would create two basic bipolar models, one without the presence of terrorist actors and the other with such presence. Now, suppose that we were also interested in the ratio of power between blocs in these systems. More exactly, suppose that we were to hypothesize that in bipolar systems with terrorist actors, power management is more effective if the ratio between blocs is equal and than if it is unequal. To evaluate this hypothesis, we would turn to the redefined heterosymmetrical and heteroasymmetrical models described earlier.

Similarly, if we were interested in discovering the effects of terrorist presence on power management in multipolar systems, we might advance the following hypothesis: The effectiveness of power management in multipolar systems decreases as terrorist actors enter the scene. To begin to explore this hypothesis we would examine two forms of multipolarity, one without terrorist actors and the other with such actors. And if we were to hypothesize further that when terrorist actors are present, power management is more effective if the ratio of power between national actors is equal than if it is unequal, the second multipolar model would be subdivided. Of the resultant two models, one would have an equal ratio of power and the other an unequal ratio.

If we were interested in the relative effects of terrorist actors on power management in bipolar and multipolar systems, we would hypothesize a particular relationship comparing these effects. To investigate this hypothesis, it would be necessary to explore at least two basic models: a bipolar one and a multipolar one, each with the presence of terrorist actors. If we were to modify the hypothesis by introducing ratio of power (between blocs or national actors) as an intervening variable, we would explore at least four basic models. This is because each original model would be subdivided according to whether the ratio were equal or unequal. If ratio of power were treated trichotomously, we would explore six basic models. Here, each original model would be subdivided according to whether the ratio were equal, mixed, or unequal.

We might also be concerned with extent of terrorist power in various systems. For example, if we were interested in the connection between such extent and power management, we might explore various subsets of the basic bipolar or multipolar models. These models would differ from each other according to the extent of terrorist power. If this intervening variable is treated dichotomously (large extent, small extent) we are left to explore four structural models. If it is treated trichotomously, each basic model would be described as equal or unequal. If it is treated trichotomously, each basic model would be equal, mixed, unequal. However it is treated, the resultant models would then be broken down, as before, according to the extent of terrorist power. Where this extent is treated as large, moderate, or small, this may mean the exploration of as many as six models for the bipolar case and nine for the multipolar one. These models might also be used for comparisons between bipolar and multipolar world systems.

Finally, if we were interested in the transmutation of decentralized global politics into a system of collective security, we might hypothesize a particular relationship between structure and collective security success. For example, it might be hypothesized that bipolar world systems are more favorable to the success of collective security than multipolar ones. To explore this hypothesis would require the creation of the basic bipolar and multipolar models.

Let us actually begin to investigate the hypothesis and see where it leads us. This requires consideration of the basic bipolar and multipolar models. Once again, it suggests that bipolar world systems are more conducive to collective security success than multipolar ones.

Why should this be the case? A comparison of the two models indicates a smaller number of "peripheries" in the bipolar case. This implies a decline in uncertainty—a decline that makes it easier for any national actor to determine the reciprocal behavior of other national actors. For an actor to decide that compliance with collective security dictates is a gainful course of action, it must believe that its own compliance will be paralleled by the compliance of a critical number of other actors. The bipolar model is also characterized by two leading national actors with preeminent power positions. This fact tends to reduce the number of individual national decisions needed for general compliance with collective security requirements. Hence, so long as the leading actors themselves are partial to collective security, their preeminence makes collective security success more likely.

Now, within the bipolar class of cases, further distinctions may be made. For example, we might hypothesize that tight bipolarity is even more favorable to collective security success than loose bipolarity. To explore this hypothesis, we must create tight and loose bipolar models. These subsets of bipolarity differ from each other in that the loose form contains a number of national actors that exist apart from the membership of the two blocs.

Why should tight bipolarity be favored? A comparison of the two bipolar forms indicates that the shift from tight to loose conditions frees an increasing number of national actors to strive for security privately rather than collectively. Such a shift has the effect of increasing the effective number of independent national actors. This shift also means that national actors may move freely between poles in cementing alliances. This broadens the number of possible interaction opportunities between these actors. As a result, the power of the leading actors is diminished. So long as such power is judged helpful to collective security success, the shift from tight to loose bipolarity must be regretted. In this case it makes it more difficult for the leading actors to ensure the compliance of other national actors.

Finally, a distinction might even be introduced into the tight bipolar class of cases. This distinction concerns the ratio of power between blocs. It appears plausible to hypothesize that within the tight bipolar category, an equal ratio of power between blocs is preferable to an unequal ratio. This is because an inequality of power between poles may offer an incentive to the more powerful bloc to magnify the advantages of private rather than collective security. To explore this hypothesis, we would have to create two subsets of the tight bipolar universe, with the differences between them being the ratio of power between blocs.

We have advanced the case for new structural models of world politics. These models would take theoretical account of terrorist actors. They could be constructed without abandoning prevailing conceptualizations such as bipolarity or multipolarity, but simply by introducing terrorist actors into these conceptualizations. This would have the effect of subdividing basic models into more complex ones.

With such models in hand, scholars might offer far more accurate representations of world politics. And they might use these representatives to examine a variety of important hypotheses relating to the requirements of planetization. As in the cases already mentioned, these hypotheses might concern the power management or war-avoidance features of global systems. Or they might concern other important dependent variables such as system transformation, stability, or national power. *Whatever* the subject to be explained, these new structural models would be apt to yield more productive insights into elements of counter–nuclear terrorism.

Not only would these models be useful for investigating certain extant hypotheses, but they might also suggest interesting hypotheses in the first place. Whereas it is true that the selection of models for investigation must depend upon the particular hypothesis in question, and that— strictly speaking—models *follow* hypotheses, the models might raise additional new hypotheses for later inquiry. In the course of investigating a new structural model derived from the hypothesis of the moment, the analyst may become aware of the new patterns and relationships that yield still more hypotheses and perhaps even more models. Hence, new structural models serve a dual role: They provide the context for exploring various hypotheses and they inspire the creation of new hypotheses. Both roles encourage the development of a more comprehensive and coherent system of counter-nuclear-terrorist theory.

In view of the urgency of the danger of nuclear terrorism, an improved system of theory represents the necessary first step to planetization. Without such a system of theory there can be no promising attempts to reorder the planet, no movement toward purposeful control of the search for new global forms.

Process

The second design dimension to be considered here concerns the processes of global power management. Although there are an extraordinary variety of conceivable arrangements for managing global power, three basic types of arrangement come immediately to mind: balance of power, collective security, and world government. These types are defined in terms of the degree of centralization exhibited. Hence, the balance of power system is the least centralized, the world government system is the most centralized, and collective security falls in between the two polar forms.[10]

Typically, scholars have argued for the advantages of increasing centralization. Such arguments derive from the assumption that the actors in world politics cannot coexist peacefully without an authority above them. From Dante in the fourteenth century to Grenville Clark and Louis Sohn, Richard Falk, and Saul Mendlovitz in the twentieth, the idea has held sway that world leaders must replace anarchy in world politics with the conditions of civil order.[11]

Although it is by no means self-evident that the effectiveness of power management parallels increasing centralization, it is certain that world leaders seeking planetization would opt for a replacement for the existing balance of power arrangement. In the existing arrangement, states are confronted with the very condition that impels them to look for alternatives: a configuration of forces wherein states define their own interests in competitive terms and in which security is mistakenly identified with the improvement or preservation of relative power position. This configuration is bound to break down calamitously in the not-too-distant future.

This brings world leaders and scholars contemplating process changes to collective security models of world order. Here, the ultimate right to make decisions concerning the use of international force is transferred from individual states to some specially established center of sovereign authority, while the actual instruments of force remain exclusively at the level of individual states. It is a condition in which the prerogative to use international force is unsupported by force.

How are world leaders and scholars likely to react to this kind of process alternative? Upon inspecting the collective security arrangement, its central problem becomes immediately apparent. Calculating that the benefits of compliance with collective security system directives are outweighed by the costs unless a condition of *general* compliance is anticipated, each state is apt to continue its reliance upon private methods of security seeking. After all, the absence of force in collective security repositories will raise grave doubts about the reciprocal compliance of every other state.

This does not mean, however, that collective security can never succeed. There are a variety of design changes that might seriously affect the decisional calculi of states, causing them to develop far greater confidence in the belief that their own prospective compliance with collective security directives would be generally paralleled.

What are these changes? They include a diminished number of actors, homogeneity as to type of actor and state government, "status quo" rather than "revolutionary-modernizing" actors, and a tight condition of bipolarity in which the ratio of power between the two blocs is roughly equal. In principle, these alterations might contribute importantly to overcoming the central impediment to collective security success: the understanding of states that their own willingness to seek security cooperatively rather than competitively will not be widely enough imitated. In fact, however, such alterations would be very difficult to produce by leaders and scholars contemplating planetary redesign along collective security lines.

Finally, scholars and world leaders thinking about planetary redesign in process terms might settle upon one form or another of world government. To do so would be to place themselves squarely in the tradition of the most heavily favored orientation to world peace. It does not mean, however, that they would certainly be opting for the most effective form of global power management. Contrary to widely held opinion, a condition of world government is not self-evidently better than less-centralized configurations. The requirements of effective war prevention are extraordinarily complex, and each particular conception of world government must be examined on its own unique merits.

Whatever the peculiar nuances of a world government process, each instance of this class of cases is characterized by the same essential distribution of force and sovereign authority. That is, the ultimate right to make decisions concerning international force is the property of some specially established global center that is endowed with some measure of force. Unlike the collective security model, therefore, sovereign directives emanating from the central authority in a world government situation *are* supported by force.

How effective is power management in such a system? Is it necessarily more effective than in the collective security system, as is usually believed? Upon inspection, statesmen and scholars will quickly perceive an important difference between the two kinds of centralized arrangements for managing world power. This difference is that the central authority in the world government system possesses some force of its own, and that world government is thus apt to be a more propitious circumstance for undercutting the tragedy of the commons. As central force now exists to enforce compliance, each state is presumably less uncertain about the willingness of other states to comply. Hence, each state is more willing to regard compliance with the dictates of centralized management as a potentially gainful course of action.

Taken by itself, however, the existence of a central force repository is insufficient to ensure widespread compliance. National decision makers must also believe that these forces are generally held to be (1) sufficiently invulnerable to first-strike attack and (2) capable of penetrating a would-be aggressor's active defenses. If these traits are in doubt, the deterrent quality of centralized forces dissolves.

Moreover, however large, powerful, and invulnerable these centralized forces might appear, their controlling authorities must also be judged willing to use them. For states to believe in the deterrent effectiveness of a specially constituted central authority, and hence in that authority's ability to overcome "the tragedy of the commons," they must perceive that that authority is not only widely recognized as capable of delivering an unacceptably damaging retaliatory strike, but that it is also generally believed willing to do so. Perceived willingness, then, is an essential ingredient of the world government center's deterrence posture.

From what we have just discussed, world leaders and scholars exploring the desirability of a world government approach to world security would be mistaken to assume that increasing global centralization is self-evidently worthwhile. Even if a specially constituted central authority were to possess some force of its own, successful deterrence need not be assured. This is because such success requires the belief of states that the central authority is willing to carry out its threats of retaliation and that its forces are sufficiently invulnerable to preemptive attacks or to subsequent attempts at active defense. These requirements are exceedingly complex. They must not be overlooked by prospective designers of an alternative world order.

Context

A final dimension to be considered by world leaders and scholars groping toward planetization concerns the prevailing weapons technology context of world politics. Although there are a great many ways in which global patterns may be characterized along this particular dimension, the most obvious and important one centers on the distinction between conventional and nuclear weapons. In short, system-directed planetary designers might contemplate the most propitious kind of distribution of the instruments of two qualitatively distinct powers of destruction.

From what we already know, world leaders must take steps to curtail the proliferation of nuclear weapons. With such proliferation, the world system moves closer and closer to the true Hobbesian state of nature— a condition of "dreadful equality" in which "the weakest has strength enough to kill the strongest." This condition, of course, has frighteningly destabilizing implications for global security. Consider the following five points concerning the requirements and limitations of nuclear deterrence:

1. The tremendous power of destruction that accompanies a nuclear-weapons capability does not automatically bestow safety from aggression. The success of nuclear deterrence rests not only upon perceptions of

explosive power, but also upon perceptions of willingness to use such power. Such willingness may not always be present. And even where it is present, instances might arise in which prospective aggressors fail to recognize it. In these instances, nuclear deterrence could fail even though a nuclear-weapons state had actually committed itself to threat fulfillment. With the proliferation of nuclear weapons, this sort of failure would become increasingly likely.

2. The success of nuclear deterrence also requires secure nuclear retaliatory forces, that is, forces that are not susceptible to nullification by a first-strike attack. The condition of secure nuclear forces, however, is not only difficult to satisfy, it is especially difficult in the case of prospective members of the nuclear club. It follows that the prospect of preemptive or first-strike attacks would be intolerably high in a world with an expanding number of nuclear-weapons states. Moreover, to protect against preemption, new nuclear powers would almost certainly adopt hair-trigger and launch-on-warning strategies for weapons release that would heighten the hazards of accidental or inadvertent firings.

3. The greater the number of nuclear powers, the greater the probability of catastrophic nuclear accidents or accidental nuclear wars. This is the case not only because of the multiplication of present risks, but also because these risks are certain to be aggravated in a proliferated global context. New nuclear powers would be unlikely to adopt the sophisticated sorts of redundant safeguards against inadvertent firings that are now in use by the superpowers. New nuclear powers would also be more apt to initiate imprecise command/control procedures that might render the proper locus of authority difficult to determine.

4. The greater the number of nuclear powers, the greater the likelihood of nuclear-weapons use by unauthorized personnel. New nuclear powers would be apt to use fewer, less sophisticated safeguards against unauthorized use than do the superpowers. And they might also increase the number of decision makers who are authorized to use nuclear weapons.

5. The greater the number of nuclear powers, the greater the probability of nuclear-weapons use by irrational national leaders. Should irrational leaders get hold of nuclear weapons, they might very well initiate nuclear strikes against other nuclear-weapons states even though enormously destructive or even annihilating retaliation were anticipated. Here, the so-called logic of nuclear deterrence would break down completely and, perhaps, irretrievably.[12]

Understanding these points, leaders and scholars examining the context design dimension must begin to identify strategies for halting the spread of nuclear weapons. As we have already seen, such strategies must concern not only the horizontal spread of nuclear weapons to states that are not yet members of the nuclear club, but also the vertical spread that is implied by the U.S.-Soviet strategic arms race. Although some progress is now under way, a great deal still remains to be done.

Conclusion

We have now seen how an improved system of world order—a system of planetization that is essential to freedom from nuclear terrorism—might be conceptualized using three design dimensions. Of course, it is one thing to talk about the conceptualization of alternative global societies and another to take actual steps toward the implementation of such societies. Nevertheless, however infeasible it might appear, the creation of a new world order within which states can begin to maximize their preferences cooperatively rather than competitively is integral to avoiding nuclear terrorism. There is no other way. To stay within the present system of world order—the time-dishonored *bellum omnes contra omnes*—is certainly more feasible, but it is hardly more realistic as this system cannot last out the century.

What can be done to hasten the serious exploration of alternative world futures and—ultimately—to implement appropriate forms of system transformation? For a beginning, national leaders must begin to expand upon the principles articulated by former president Jimmy Carter in his speech at the University of Notre Dame. "For too many years, we have been willing to adopt the flawed and erroneous principles and tactics of our adversaries, sometimes abandoning our own values for theirs. We have fought fire with fire, never thinking that fire is better quenched with water. This approach failed, with Vietnam the best example of its intellectual and moral poverty."[13] To succeed in such expansion, world leaders must learn to understand and accept the inescapable interrelatedness of their national destinies.

At the moment, world leaders continue to act on the mistaken assumption that their longstanding foreign policies of "everyone for himself" can be conducted indefinitely without fatal consequences. To replace this sort of understanding with a new affirmation of global singularity and solidarity would represent a natural starting point for the essential restructuring of national and world political life. As far as effective strategies of counter–nuclear terrorism are concerned, there is no better starting point.

States, like individual persons, are cemented to each other not by haphazard aggregation, but by the certainty of their basic interdependence. Beneath the diversities of a seemingly fractionated world, there exists a basic oneness. With this manifestation of the "one in the many," states may begin to aim at particular goals and objectives in harmony with all other states. With an integral vision sparked by the impulse of global solidarity, states may begin to produce refinements in their relationships that can bring them back from the brink. Unlike anything else, this vision can endow the search for planetization and freedom from nuclear terrorism with real potency.

The Behavioral Underpinnings

In the final analysis, the creation of an improved world order—one characterized, inter alia, by a reduced risk of nuclear terrorism—will require a national and international move toward *personhood*. Rejecting the idea that our self-worth is tied inextricably to our membership in particular states, we must learn to discover genuine sources of self-affirmation and self-esteem *within ourselves*. Daring to look our approaching disappearance in the face, we may then progress beyond the desolate clairvoyance of realpolitik to a new global politics of reason and hope.

How shall we begin this process of transformation? In the United States there is no quick fix to the problem of personhood, no magic bullet that can destroy the invidious pathology in our national body politic. Rather, faced with a system of international relations that offers only endless infamy, we must learn to draw meaning from outside the cold, metallic surfaces of the state. Acknowledging our captivity by endless cycles of useless production and consumption, we must begin to replace fraudulent definitions of success with authentic measures of private and national growth.

Inventiveness must take new forms. Revolted by the herd and its mouthpieces, we must learn to understand our disorder. A collapsing civilization compromises with its disease, cherishes the infectious pathology. We, however, must choose to rebel, attacking the false communion of national and international life with our growth as individuals.

For the moment, Hegel is triumphant! Everywhere the highest duty is fulfilled as a member of the state. Everywhere the state acts as the true self, bending "mere individuals" to the general will. Absorbing and cancelling individuality, every state is worshipped as a manifestation of the "absolute spirit." The resultant condition is not only loveless; it is the starting point for terrorism.

In Herman Hesse's *Demian,* the narrator, Emil Sinclair, intones, "I realize today that nothing in the world is more distasteful to a man than to take the path that leads to himself." Yet, it is only when entire nations overcome such distaste and flee the fear of their own inwardness that life can be protected from political violence. Discarding the sounds and the rituals of methodically rehearsed loyalties, these individuals can destroy the lethal reign of the herd. Only then will we be really free from the threat of nuclear terrorism.

Notes

Chapter 1

1. On December 9, 1985, the UN General Assembly unanimously adopted a resolution condemning all acts of terrorism as "criminal." Never before had the assembly adopted such a comprehensive resolution on this question. Yet the issue of particular acts that actually constitute terrorism is still left unresolved, except for acts that were criminalized by previous conventions, such as hijacking and hostage-taking attacks on internationally protected persons. Even in these cases the practical problem of gaining support for the "extradite-or-prosecute" formula remains a serious impediment to effective counterterrorism. On conventional law in force regarding terrorism, see for example the 1963 Tokyo Convention, the 1970 Hague Convention, and the 1971 Montreal Convention. See also the 1979 International Convention Against the Taking of Hostages, the 1961 Vienna Convention on Diplomatic Relations, the 1973 Convention on the Prevention and Punishment of Crimes Against Internationally Protected Persons, Including Diplomatic Agents, and the 1975 Helsinki Final Act.

2. See United Nations, General Assembly, *Official Records,* 28th Session, *Report of the Ad Hoc Committee on International Terrorism,* Suppl. 28 (A/9028), 1973, p. 21.

3. Article 3 (g) states: "The sending by or on behalf of a State of armed bands, groups, irregulars or mercenaries, which carry out acts of armed force against another State of such gravity as to amount to the acts listed above, or its substantial involvement therein." Cited in Benjamin B. Ferencz, *Defining International Aggression: The Search for World Peace,* vol. 2 (New York: Oceana, 1975), p. 17.

4. On October 24, 1970, the General Assembly adopted the following Declaration on Principles of International Law Concerning Friendly Relations and Cooperation Among States: "Every State has the duty to refrain from organizing, instigating, assisting or participating in acts of civil strife or terrorist acts in another State or acquiescing in organized activities within its territory directed towards the commission of such acts, when the acts referred to in the present paragraph involve a threat or use of force." However, this same Declaration includes even greater emphasis on the "principle of equal rights and self-determination of peoples." "Every state has the duty to refrain from any forcible action which deprives people referred to above in the elaboration of the present principles of their right to self-determination and freedom and independence. In their actions against, and resistance to, such forcible action in pursuit of the exercise of their right to self-determination, such peoples are entitled to seek

and to receive support in accordance with the purposes and principles of the Charter." See *Yearbook of the United Nations 1970* (New York: UN, Office of Public Information, 1971), pp. 790–791.

5. See Ferencz, *Defining International Aggression,* p. 18.

6. Cited by Walter Laqueur, ed., *The Terrorism Reader: A Historical Anthology from Aristotle to the IRA and the PLO* (New York: New American Library, 1978), p. 16.

7. See Sergey Nechaev, *Catechism of the Revolutionist,* 1869, cited in Laqueur, *The Terrorism Reader,* p. 68.

8. See Curtis Bill Pepper, "The Possessed," *New York Times Magazine,* February 18, 1979, p. 32.

9. However, even those terrorist groups with distinctly identifiable political objectives must be distinguished from the "classical" revolutionary. The revolutionary seeks to "seize power," usually by a frontal assault on the centers of political control. Using such methods as the general strike and the occupation of military, police, and industrial bases, he/she avoids random actions against peripheral targets. Force is used, but almost never with deliberation against innocent parties.

10. Evidence of this phenomenon may be found in the successes of several Middle Eastern terrorist groups against Americans abroad and the resultant reduction of U.S. tourism in Europe and elsewhere.

11. See Hannah Arendt, *On Violence* (New York: Harcourt Brace and World, 1970), p. 5.

12. In this connection, it should be pointed out that Marx did not believe in individual terrorism and that both Lenin and Trotsky had serious reservations about indiscriminate terrorism. Contemporary Communist parties maintain a doctrinal opposition to most terror tactics and generally avoid such tactics in pursuit of their objectives. In fact, such groups as the Italian Red Brigades are largely a response to the "revisionism" of established Communist parties, and there is considerable irony in their association of terrorism with a "true communism."

13. Curiously, recent official U.S. government definitions of terrorism do not allow for "just cause." According to a September 1984 definition offered by the Department of State, Bureau of Public Affairs, "Terrorism is the use or threatened use of violence for political purposes to create a state of fear that will aid in extorting, coercing, intimidating or otherwise causing individuals and groups to alter their behavior." (See "International Terrorism," GIST series). By this definition, of course, the eighteenth-century revolutionary insurgency that led to the creation of the United States was *pure terrorism.* Similarly, the U.S.-supported contras are also terrorists by this definition.

14. On the particular crime of apartheid, see United Nations, General Assembly, *Official Records, 28, International Convention on the Suppression and Punishment of the Crime of Apartheid,* entered into force July 18, 1976, G.A. Res. 3068, Suppl. 30 (A/9030), 1974. See also idem, *Official Records, 20, International Convention on the Elimination of All Forms of Racial Discrimination,* entered into force Jan. 4, 1969, G.A. Res. 2160A, Suppl. 14 (A/6014), 1966.

15. See Octavio Paz, "Latin America and Democracy," in *Democracy and Dictatorship in Latin America,* a special publication of the Foundation for Independent Study of Social Ideas (New York, 1982), p. 13.

16. Ibid., p. 9.

Chapter 2

1. In the recent judgment of the International Task Force on Prevention of Nuclear Terrorism, a project of the Nuclear Control Institute, the probability of nuclear terrorism is increasing due to the following confluence of factors:

- the growing incidence, sophistication, and lethality of conventional forms of terrorism, often to increase shock value;
- apparent evidence of state support, even sponsorship, of terrorist groups;
- the storing and deploying of nuclear weapons in areas of intense terrorist activity;
- an increasing number of potential targets in civil nuclear programs—in particular facilities and shipments in which plutonium and uranium, in forms suitable for use in weapons, are present;
- potential black and gray markets in nuclear equipment and materials.

See *Report of the International Task Force on Prevention of Nuclear Terrorism,* June 25, 1986, a project of the Nuclear Control Institute, Washington, D.C., (hereinafter cited as *Report*), p. 1.

2. Ibid.

3. Ibid., p. 7. Significantly, a number of tactical nuclear weapons stored in the United States do not have PALs.

4. See George Schultz, "Low-Intensity Warfare: The Challenge of Ambiguity," U.S., Department of State, Bureau of Public Affairs, Current Policy No. 783 (Washington, D.C., January 15, 1986), p. 4.

5. See Thomas Davies, "Terrorism's Nuclear Potential: What Might The Means and Targets Be?" (Paper presented at the Conference on International Terrorism: The Nuclear Dimension, Nuclear Control Institute, Washington, D.C., June 1985, p. 3.

6. *Report,* p. 7.

7. See U.S., Congress, House, Committee on Foreign Affairs, Subcommittee on International Security and Scientific Affairs, Statement by Bernard J. O'Keefe, chairman, EG&G, Inc., *Legislation to Combat International Terrorism; Hearings,* 98th Cong. November 9, 1983, p. 13.

8. Davies, "Terrorism's Nuclear Potential," pp. 2–3.

9. See *Legislation to Combat International Terrorism: Hearings,* p. 2.

10. *Report,* p. 12. The Atomic Energy Act of 1954 and the Energy Reorganization Act of 1974 direct the NRC to regulate the safeguards provided by certain nuclear facilities and activities to assure protection of the public and national defense. The NRC coordinates its safeguards programs and hypothetical design basis threats with the Department of Energy. To accomplish its responsibilities, the NRC seeks to ensure that measures are taken to "deter, prevent, or respond to the unauthorized possession or use of significant quantities of

special nuclear material through theft or diversion, and to protect against radiological sabotage of certain nuclear facilities. In general, safeguards for fuel cycle facilities and nonpower reactors emphasize protection against theft or diversion of special nuclear material (SNM), while those for power reactors stress protection against radiological sabotage. (SNM and Strategic Special Nuclear Materials, or SSNM, are shorthand for technical definitions of various kinds of nuclear materials, different quantities thereof, and different degrees of enrichment. In general, SSNM is highly enriched uranium or plutonium.)" See U.S. Nuclear Regulatory Commission, *1984 Annual Report,* NUREG—1145 (Washington, D.C.: Government Printing Office, transmitted to the president on June 12, 1985), p. 77. Chapter 6 of this report is titled "Safeguards."

11. *Report,* p. 12.

12. Ibid.

13. In some cases, however, foreign safeguards are already more effective than our own. For example, a system now being used in West Germany, Switzerland, and other Western European countries is designed to ensure flooding of a reactor core with cooling water even if terrorists, with the aid of insiders, take over a control room and attempt to cause a core meltdown. This bunkered emergency core cooling system, not presently required by the U.S. Nuclear Regulatory Commission for U.S. reactors, goes into operation automatically and can be overriden only from controls within a penetration-resistant bunker isolated from the rest of the plant. See *Report,* p. 12. For a complete list of U.S. federal regulations covering the physical protection of plants and materials, see U.S., Office of the Federal Register, *Code of Federal Regulations: Energy,* 10, Parts 0 to 199, Revised as of January 1, 1986 (Washington, D.C.: Government Printing Office, 1986), Part 73, "Physical Protection of Plants and Materials," pp. 750–807.

14. Despite delays affecting many reprocessing projects, it has been estimated that by the year 2000 the total amount of separated "civilian" plutonium in the West will amount to as much as 365 tons. See David A. V. Fischer, "The Challenge of Nuclear Safeguards," *Bulletin of the Atomic Scientists* 42, no. 6 (June/July 1986): 31.

15. Civilian nuclear power reactors are operated today almost exclusively on a "once-through" fuel cycle in which weapons-usable material is never easily accessible. The spent fuel discharged from the reactor is not reprocessed, so that the contained plutonium and uranium remain locked with the highly radioactive fission products.

16. See *Report,* p. 9.

17. See Harold A. Feiveson, Frank von Hippel, and David Albright, "Breaking the Fuel/Weapons Connection," *Bulletin of the Atomic Scientists* 42, no. 3 (March 1986); 28.

18. U.S., Congress, Office of Technology Assessment, *Nuclear Proliferation and Safeguards* (New York: Praeger, 1977). See U.S., Congress, Senate, Committee on Governmental Affairs, *Hearings: An Act To Combat International Terrorism,* 95th Cong., 2nd sess., January 23–March 23, 1978 (hereinafter cited as *Hearings*), pp. 250–251.

19. See Mason Willrich and Theodore B. Taylor, *Nuclear Theft: Risks and Safeguards* (Cambridge, Mass.: Ballinger, 1974), p. 1.

20. *Hearings,* p. 266.

21. Ibid., p. 267.

22. See *Princeton Alumni Weekly,* October 25, 1976.

23. See "Two Small U.S. Journals Have Printed Article on Building A-Bombs," *New York Times,* March 11, 1979, p. 21.

24. See "Bomb Class Added to College Catalog," *Denver Post,* October 2, 1977.

25. *Hearings,* March 22, 1978, pp. 275–276.

26. See *Report,* p. 2.

27. See, for example, Bennett Ramberg, "Nuclear Plants—Military Hostages?" *Bulletin of the Atomic Scientists* 42, no. 3 (March 1986): 17–21; Daniel Hirsch, Stephanie Murphy, and Bennett Ramberg, "Protecting Reactors From Terrorists," ibid., pp. 22–25; and Daniel Hirsch, Bennett Ramberg, and Stephanie Murphy, *Nuclear Terrorism: A Growing Threat,* A report to the Safeguards and Security Subcommittee, Advisory Committee on Reactor Safeguards, U.S. Nuclear Regulatory Commission, May 7, 1985, SPNP-85-F-1.

28. See Davies, "Terrorism's Nuclear Potential," pp. 9–10.

29. Ibid., p. 10.

30. See *Report,* pp. 10–11.

31. A prominent exception to the terrorist doctrine of indiscriminacy is Carlos Marighella's *Minimanual of the Urban Guerrilla.* According to Marighella, a Brazilian Communist who established the terrorist organization Action for National Liberation (ALN), the urban guerrilla "follows a political goal and only attacks the government, the big capitalists, and the foreign imperialists, particularly North Americans." See Walter Laqueur, ed., *The Guerrilla Reader* (New York: New American Library, 1977), excerpt from the *Minimanual,* p. 219. Similarly, Abraham Guillen, one of the principal theoreticians of urban guerrilla tactics, argued that the creation of a general climate of terror is both wrong and impolitic: "A popular army that resorts to unnecessary violence, that is not a symbol of justice, equity, liberty, and security, cannot win popular support in the struggle against a dehumanized tyranny." From "Urban Guerrilla Strategy," in Laqueur, *The Guerrilla Reader,* p. 234.

32. See Yehoshafat Harkabi, "Al Fatah's Doctrine," in Walter Laqueur, ed., *The Terrorism Reader* (New York: New American Library, 1978), p. 151.

33. Ibid., p. 150.

34. See Mikhail Bakhunin, *Neskolko slov k molodym bratyam v Rossii,* Geneva, 1869, cited in Laqueur, *The Terrorism Reader,* p. 65.

35. See Guillen, "Urban Guerrilla Strategy," p. 233.

36. See Herbert Marcuse, *Counterrevolution and Revolt* (Boston: Beacon Press, 1972), p. 52.

37. See Gerald Priestland, *The Future of Violence* (London: Hamish Hamilton, 1974), p. 155.

38. See Charles A. Russell et al., "Out-Inventing the Terrorist," reprinted in *Hearings,* p. 832.

39. Ibid.

40. It should be pointed out, however, that there are classical writings on international law that support intervention on humanitarian grounds. For example, Grotius regarded it as a duty of foreign nations to intervene when "a tyrant practices atrocities towards his subjects" (Book 2 of *The Law of War and Peace*). And Pufendort expressed a similar idea in Book 8 of his *The Law of Nature and Nations*. But the modern international law of human rights, although rejecting an absolute doctrine of freedom from external interference, does not countenance the support of terrorist violence by certain states against other states.

41. See Laqueur, *The Terrorism Reader,* p. 119.

42. See Abstract of Rand Paper, P-5261, "International Terrorism: A New Kind of Warfare," June 1974, 13 pp., cited in *A Bibliography of Selected Rand Publications,* January 1977, p. 2.

43. See Brian Jenkins, *International Terrorism: A New Mode of Conflict,* Research Paper No. 48, California Seminar on Arms Control and Foreign Policy (Los Angeles: Crescent Publications, 1975), p. 21.

44. See report by Commodore R. E. Bigney, USN, et al., Defense Documentation Center, Defense Supply Agency, June 3, 1974, p. 41.

45. See Hersch Lauterpacht, *International Law,* vol. 3., *The Law of Peace,* parts 2–6 (Cambridge: Cambridge University Press, 1977), p. 274. Today the longstanding customary prohibition against foreign support for lawless insurgencies is codified in the UN charter and in the authoritative interpretation of that multilateral treaty in Article 1 and Article 3(g) of the 1974 UN General Assembly Definition of Aggression.

Chapter 3

1. See testimony by Dr. Theodore B. Taylor, March 22, 1978, in U.S., Congress, Senate, Committee on Governmental Affairs, *Hearings: An Act to Combat International Terrorism,* 95th Cong., 2nd sess., January 23–March 23, 1978 (hereinafter cited as *Hearings*), p. 266.

2. See testimony by Dimitri A. Rotow, March 22, 1978, *Hearings,* p. 273.

3. See Mason Willrich and Theodore B. Taylor, *Nuclear Theft: Risks and Safeguards* (Cambridge, Mass.: Ballinger, 1974), p. 22.

4. *Report of the International Task Force on Prevention of Nuclear Terrorism,* June 25, 1986, a project of the Nuclear Control Institute, Washington, D.C. (hereinafter cited as *Report*), p. 6.

5. See Arthur Manfredi, Robert Shuey, Richard Preece, Robert Sutter, and Warren Donnelly, "Ballistic Missile Proliferation Potential in the Third World," Congressional Research Service, Library of Congress, Washington, D.C., April 1986, 37 pp.

6. See U.S., Congress, Office of Technology Assessment, *Nuclear Proliferation and Safeguards* (New York: Praeger, 1977), p. 146.

7. See Willrich and Taylor, *Nuclear Theft: Risks and Safeguards,* p. 27.

8. Ibid. On June 6, 1986, Dr. Jack Geiger, president of Physicians for Social Responsibility, visited Moscow Hospital No. 6 "to see some of the still-surviving

victims of the disaster at Chernobyl, to review their medical care, and to learn of their prognoses." Here is what he observed: "I saw young men with dreadful radiation burns, peering out at me from behind the plastic shields that protected them from the certainty of death by infection. I saw others who had *not* been seriously burned, who had *not* had their bone marrow destroyed, who were visibly healthy. Yet, these were victims too—men in apparent good physical health who must live that portion of life yet left to them never knowing if, or when, their lives would be brought to premature ends by radiation-induced leukemia and other cancers. . . . There were perhaps 300 patients from Chernobyl at Moscow Hospital No. 6. Yet, this very limited nuclear accident had strained to the breaking point the medical resources of the entire Soviet Union." Taken from "A Day For Peace," printed letter from Physicians for Social Responsibility, July 1986.

9. See Edmund Faltermayer, "Exorcising the Nightmare of Reactor Meltdowns," *Fortune,* March 12, 1979, p. 82.

10. The Rasmussen Report of October 1975 is the popular description of the *Reactor Safety Study* (WASH-1400), a study sponsored by the Nuclear Regulatory Commission, Washington, D.C. See *Nuclear Power: Issues and Choices,* Report of the Nuclear Energy Policy Study Group, sponsored by the Ford Foundation, administered by the Mitre Corporation (Cambridge, Mass.: Ballinger, 1977), p. 224. For an interesting early assessment of the Rasmussen Report, see H. A. Bethe, "The Necessity of Fission Power," *Scientific American* 234, no. 1 (January 1976): 21–31.

11. See U.S. Nuclear Regulatory Commission, H. W. Lewis, chairman, *Risk Assessment Review Group Report* (Washington, D.C.: Government Printing Office, September 1978), bibliographic data sheet.

12. Ibid., p. vi.

13. Ibid.

14. Ibid., pp. viii–x.

15. See *Report,* pp. 1–2. See also *Safeguards Summary Event List* (SSEL), NUREG-0525 (Washington, D.C.: Office of Nuclear Material Safety and Safeguards, U.S. Nuclear Regulatory Commission, January 1986). This list provides brief summaries of several hundred safeguards-related events involving nuclear material or facilities regulated by the U.S. Nuclear Regulatory Commission. Events are described under the following categories: bomb-related, intrusion, missing and/or allegedly stolen, transportation, tampering/vandalism, arson, firearms, radiological sabotage, nonradiological sabotage, and miscellaneous.

16. See Daniel Hirsch, Bennett Ramberg, and Stephanie Murphy, *Nuclear Terrorism: A Growing Threat,* a report to the Safeguards and Security Subcommittee, Advisory Committee on Reactor Safeguards, U.S. Nuclear Regulatory Commission, May 7, 1985, SPNP-85-F-1, p. 2. See also Bennett Ramberg, "Nuclear Plants—Military Hostages?" *Bulletin of the Atomic Scientists* 42, no. 3 (March 1986): 17–21; and Daniel Hirsch, Stephanie Murphy, and Bennett Ramberg, "Protecting Reactors from Terrorists," ibid., pp. 22–25.

17. See Consultant Workshop, Sandia Laboratories, *Summary Report on Workshop on Sabotage Protection in Nuclear Power Plant Design,* SAND 76-0637

(Washington, D.C.: U.S. Nuclear Regulatory Commission, 1977); and Dean C. Kaul and Edward S. Sachs, *Adversary Actions in the Nuclear Fuel Cycle: I. Reference Events and Their Consequences,* SAI-121-612-7803 (Schaumburg, Ill.: Science Applications, 1977).

18. See Ramberg, "Nuclear Plants—Military Hostages?" p. 17.

19. Ibid. See also Jan Beyea, *Some Long-Term Consequences of Hypothetical Major Releases of Radioactivity to the Atmosphere from Three Mile Island,* PU/CEES No. 109, Center for Energy and Environmental Studies, Princeton University, December 1980.

20. See Andrei D. Sakharov, *Progress, Coexistence, and Intellectual Freedom* (New York: W. W. Norton, 1968), p. 37.

21. See Ruth Leger Sivard, *World Military and Social Expenditures 1985* (Washington, D.C.: World Priorities, 1985), p. 16.

22. See Bernard T. Feld, "The Consequences of Nuclear War," *Bulletin of the Atomic Scientists* 32, no. 6 (June 1976), p. 12.

23. See *Economic and Social Consequences of Nuclear Attacks on the United States,* a study prepared for U.S., Congress, Joint Committee on Defense Production (Washington, D.C.: Senate Committee on Banking, Housing, and Urban Affairs, March 1979), pp. 35–36.

24. Ibid., p. v.

25. See *Long-Term Worldwide Effects of Multiple Nuclear-Weapons Detonations,* Committee to Study the Long-Term Worldwide Effects of Multiple Nuclear-Weapon Detonations, Assembly of Mathematical and Physical Sciences, National Research Council, National Academy of Sciences, Washington, D.C., 1975.

26. *Economic and Social Consequences of Nuclear Attacks on the United States,* p. 2.

27. See Carl Sagan, *The Nuclear Winter* (Boston: Council for a Livable World Education Fund, 1983), 10 pp.

28. For additional information on nuclear winter, see Richard P. Turco, Owen B. Toon, Thomas P. Ackerman, James B. Pollack, and Carl Sagan, "The Climatic Effects of Nuclear War," *Scientific American* 251, no. 2 (August 1984): 33–43; Paul R. Ehrlich et al., "Long-Term Biological Consequences of Nuclear War," *Science* 222, no. 4630 (December 23, 1983): 1293–1300; R. P. Turco et al., "Nuclear Winter: Global Consequences of Multiple Nuclear Explosions," *Science* 222, no. 4630 (December 23, 1983): 1283–1292; Carl Sagan, "Nuclear War and Climatic Catastrophe: Some Policy Implications," *Foreign Affairs* 62, no. 2 (Winter/1983/1984): 257–292; Curt Covey et al., "Global Atmospheric Effects of Massive Smoke Injections from a Nuclear War: Results from General Circulations Model Simulations," *Nature* 308, no. 5954 (March 1, 1984): 21–25; and Sagan, *The Nuclear Winter.*

29. See *Long-Term Worldwide Effects of Multiple Nuclear-Weapons Detonations,* p. 60.

30. Ibid., p. 66.

31. Ibid., p. 85.

32. Ibid., pp. 12–13.

33. See Tom Stonier, *Nuclear Disaster* (New York: Meridian, 1964), p. 54.

34. See *Economic and Social Consequences of Nuclear Attacks on the United States,* p. 21.

35. See John Willett, ed. and trans., *Brecht on Theatre* (New York: Hill and Wang, 1964), p. 27.

Chapter 4

1. See *Extracts From Nuclear Weapons Security Primer* (Washington, D.C.: Department of Defense, April 1, 1975).

2. According to Article 6 of the Treaty on the Non-Proliferation of Nuclear Weapons, "Each of the Parties to the Treaty undertakes to pursue negotiations in good faith on effective measures relating to cessation of the nuclear arms race at an early date and to nuclear disarmament, and on a treaty on general and complete disarmament under strict and effective international control."

3. Minimum deterrence refers to a concept of reciprocal nuclear threat that is based on the ability of each superpower to inflict unacceptable damage upon the other superpower after absorbing a nuclear first strike. Unlike the rationale of this country's developing "countervailing" nuclear strategy, which ties deterrence to a nuclear warfighting capacity, minimum deterrence rests only on the maintenance of survivable and penetration-capable nuclear forces. Hence, it is linked to a targeting doctrine that stresses cities and population centers rather than military "hard" targets.

Although it is sometimes argued that minimum deterrence is not credible because any U.S. retaliation would carry an overwhelmingly high probability of all-out nuclear war, this argument fails to understand that any U.S. counterforce reprisal would carry the same risks. This is the case because the "collateral damage" from such counterforce attacks would include tens of millions of fatalities and because a rational Soviet adversary could not possibly afford to conform to U.S. strategic rules concerning a "limited" nuclear war. Indeed, Soviet policy continues to threaten the United States with all-out nuclear war once U.S. counterforce reprisals have been launched. It follows that the alleged "flexibility" of current U.S. nuclear strategy is illusory, offering no advantages over a strategy of minimum deterrence.

Current nuclear strategy does, however, carry serious comparative disadvantages. Because the U.S. search for a nuclear warfighting capacity heightens Soviet fears of first strike by the United States, this search significantly degrades this country's security. Moreover, U.S. nuclear weapons that are counterforce targeted to conform to nuclear warfighting doctrines of deterrence will have a measurably reduced deterrent effect because it is clear that their use in a second strike would produce less damage to the USSR than would extensive countervalue attacks.

4. Amidst the din and controversy surrounding the cruise and Pershing II deployments, our government has always overlooked the most vital point: These missiles could never actually be used in retaliation by a rational president of the United States. In the event of a Soviet/Warsaw Pact conventional attack against Western Europe—the scenario that gives rise to the NATO Euromissile deployments—a reprisal by any number of the projected 572 missiles directed

against the Soviet homeland would lead to an all-out nuclear war. Consequently, the threat to use these missiles to deter such an attack is wholly incredible. It could be argued in response that this threat might still be credible if the Soviets believed the U.S. president to be irrational, but if this were indeed the case the Soviets would have an irresistible and continuing incentive to strike first.

What if the Soviets should launch their nuclear weapons as a first offensive move of war? In such a case, the cruise and Pershing II missiles would also prove useless because they would add nothing to our existing strategic capabilities. Whatever feeble damage-limitation benefits might accrue to the United States from its arsenal of counterforce-targeted nuclear weapons, they would not be improved by the firing of up to 572 new medium-range missiles. This is the case because there would be very little of the United States left to protect after the first round of Soviet attacks had been absorbed. Moreover, the United States doesn't even target Soviet submarine-launched ballistic missiles.

Why, then, did we deploy the new weapons? From the Soviet point of view, the only rational explanation must seem to lie in U.S. plans for a preemptive attack against their nuclear forces. Although the new missiles would, by themselves, do nothing to enhance the prospects for such an attack, it is conceivable that they would be judged useful to preemption in conjunction with existing Triad forces—ICBMs, SLBMs (submarine-launched ballistic missiles), and bombers. This judgment would follow from the Pershing IIs' potential to strike such protected targets as command bunkers and nuclear storage sites in the western USSR less than ten minutes after launch. And this entire first-strike appraisal must be considered together with parallel U.S. plans for the MX, antisatellite (ASAT) weapons, ballistic missile defense (BMD), and improved civil defense.

We see, therefore, that because the Euromissile deployment is entirely useless as a deterrent, it suggests U.S. first-strike intentions to the Soviets. Such intentions are almost certainly not the purpose of these new weapons. All that matters, however, are Soviet perceptions.

5. Nuclear-freeze resolutions began in Massachusetts in November 1980. By 1984 such resolutions had been passed by 370 cities and 71 county councils throughout the United States. During May and June 1986 local freeze groups across the country carried out freeze walks. Current plans call for a new gathering of signatures calling for a nuclear warhead test ban as a first step toward an effective freeze.

6. See L. R. Beres, ed., *Security or Armageddon: Israel's Nuclear Strategy* (Lexington, Mass.: Lexington Books, 1986).

7. The International Atomic Energy Agency, which came into existence on July 29, 1957, is an independent, intergovernmental organization within the United Nations system. Despite its weaknesses, much has been already done to improve safeguards. The number of inspectors and inspections has almost doubled in the past five years, and in 1983 the IAEA began carrying out "surprise" inspections. To further improve its capabilities in the future, the organization will have to deal with large reprocessing and MOX (mixed oxides of uranium and plutonium) fuel fabrication plants and with emerging enrichment technologies. For more on the political and technical challenges that face the IAEA,

see David A. V. Fischer, "The Challenge of Nuclear Safeguards," *Bulletin of the Atomic Scientists* 42, no. 6 (June/July 1986): 29–33.

8. In this connection, although the nuclear states have attempted to limit the export of nuclear-weapons related materials and equipment through formal agreements, a new challenge has emerged: a "gray market" in which nuclear material and information are obtained through smuggling, exploitation of loopholes in nuclear export controls, and fraud. For information on this nuclear netherworld, see Leonard S. Spector, "The Nuclear Netherworld," *Issues in Science and Technology* 2, no. 4 (Summer 1986): 96–101.

9. Following the example of France and Great Britain, Japan, West Germany, and India have already built their own small or intermediate-scale reprocessing facilities, and Argentina, Brazil, and Pakistan are now developing reprocessing capabilities. Moreover, even where particular countries have undertaken the reprocessing of nuclear fuel from other countries as a commercial venture, large amounts of separated plutonium are to be returned to nonnuclear-weapons states. This is because the high-level radioactive waste produced by reprocessing will ultimately be returned to the countries of origin. For more on this aspect of the reprocessing of spent reactor fuel to separate the contained plutonium, see Harold A. Feiveson, Frank von Hippel, and David Albright, "Breaking the Fuel/Weapons Connection," *Bulletin of the Atomic Scientists* 42, no. 3 (March 1986): 26–31.

10. For an important assessment of the linkages between emerging nuclear power technologies and nuclear proliferation, see Warren H. Donnelly, "Some Implications of Potential New Development in Nuclear Technology for the Proliferation of Nuclear Weapons," Congressional Research Service, Library of Congress, Washington, D.C., March 17, 1986, 7 pp. (mimeo).

11. Paul Leventhal, "Getting Serious About Proliferation," *Bulletin of the Atomic Scientists* 40, no. 3 (March 1984): 9.

12. See L. R. Beres, *Reason and Realpolitik: U.S. Foreign Policy and World Order* (Lexington, Mass.: Lexington Books, 1984); and Richard Halloran, "Spread of Nuclear Arms Is Seen by 2000," *New York Times,* November 15, 1982, p. 3.

13. The third review conference for the Treaty on the Non-Proliferation of Nuclear Weapons was held in September 1985. A fifth review conference will be held in 1995 to decide whether the treaty shall continue in force indefinitely. For information on the history and background of the NPT and on the 1985 review conference, see Robert L. Beckman and Warren H. Donnelly, "The Treaty on the Non-Proliferation of Nuclear Weapons: The 1985 Review Conference and Matters of Congressional Interest," Congressional Research Service, Library of Congress, Report No. 85-80 S, Washington, D.C., April 22, 1985. For additional information on the background of the current nonproliferation regime, see Warren H. Donnelly, "The International Non-Proliferation Regime: A Brief Description of its Precursors, Present Form, and United States Support For It," Congressional Research Service, Library of Congress, Report No. 83-127 S, Washington, D.C., June 1983.

14. Outside the NPT there are still nine non-nuclear-weapons states operating nuclear plants. Of these states, five (India, Pakistan, Israel, South Africa, and

Argentina) can already, or will soon, acquire the capability to produce unsafeguarded fissile material.

15. See Thomas Merton, *The Nonviolent Alternative,* ed. Gordon C. Zahn (New York: Farrar, Straus, Giroux, 1980), p. 62. Ironically, if there should be a nuclear war, it would almost certainly *not* be because of evil motives or malevolence. The tilt toward nuclear war is not an ineradicable aspect of humankind's biological endowment, an affliction of the germ plasm to be endured with resignation. Rather, it is the product of *thoughtlessness,* the literal inability to understand the probable outcome of complex strategic interactions. In the words of Albert Camus, "What strikes me, in the midst of polemics, threats and outbursts of violence, is the fundamental good will of everyone."

16. For more on the importance of expanded U.S.-Soviet cooperation on nonproliferation, see Council on Foreign Relations, *Blocking the Spread of Nuclear Weapons: American and European Perspectives* (New York: Council on Foreign Relations, 1986), 153 pp., published in cooperation with the Centre for European Policy Studies (CEPS).

17. National security means far more than the capacity for military destructiveness. Indeed the frenzied search for sustaining and expanding this capacity has produced a continuing erosion of those elements that account for real power in world affairs. By accelerating its commitment to military priorities at the expense of social and economic needs, this country has retarded its economic development through inflation, diversion of investment, misuse of scarce materials, and misuse of human capital.

Largely because of the consequences of its enormous commitment to military spending, the United States now exports raw materials in abundance and imports more manufactured goods than it sells abroad. In striking relation to its robust expansion of military spending, the United States has created a distinct government-dependent civilian sector prone to inadequacy. Inflation and waste result from its practice of rapid obsolescence and frequent product change, as well as from unstable markets, the excessive waste characteristic of large bureaucracies beyond public control, cost plus pricing, and reduced management efficiency. Instead of being a major instrument for stimulating productivity, competitiveness, and innovation, our commitment to weapons has produced intermittent recession and a society less and less able to provide its citizens with improved conditions of living. Among ten developed nations over the past twenty years, the slowest growth in investment and manufacturing productivity has occurred in the United States and Great Britain, where military expenditures have been the highest in relation to gross national product (GNP). The best investment and productivity record has been in Japan, where the military-to-GNP ratio has been very low and where productivity has grown substantially each year.

What exactly does heavy military spending do to undermine our economic and social stability? The answer is straightforward and widely understood by economists, although it has yet to be widely appreciated by the general public. Most obviously, perhaps, heavy military spending generates a stream of buying power without producing an equivalent supply of economically useful goods for the civilian market. The excess of disposable income over available supply builds up a steady and generalized pressure on prices. The problem is exacerbated by the fact that military demand also adds directly to the pressure on prices for specific goods, especially when military purchases are directed to the commodities and labor skills in shortest supply.

Heavy military spending also preempts resources that might have been otherwise invested. While an enormous share of available public funds go to weapons, the United States ignores essential research that could develop new sources of energy, increase food production, provide better housing, and improve health, employment, and all around human well-being. These distorted priorities perpetually limit innovation and investment and thus occasion national insecurity through low growth and slow productivity gains.

18. See George Konra'd, *Antipolitics,* trans. from the Hungarian by Richard Allen (New York: Harcourt Brace Jovanavich, 1984), p. 12.

19. See Hannah Arendt, *On Violence* (New York: Harcourt Brace and World, 1970), p. 7.

20. We fear Islamic militants in the Middle East because they have chosen to fuse politics and theology. Yet, we too are captives of such a fusion. Is there really such a vast difference between Shiite crusaders seeking revenge against the "Great Satan" and the president of the United States preparing for an apocalyptic war with the "Evil Empire"? Is it entirely extraneous to our all-consuming rivalry with the Soviet Union—a rivalry that creates policies that foster terrorism against the United States—that the adversary is typically lambasted as "godless"? Spokesmen for Lebanon's Hizbollah, or Party of God, have said: "We aren't against the American people. We are against oppression and injustice." Our leaders say we have nothing against the Russian people. We merely oppose the "focus of evil" in the modern world.

Chapter 5

1. According to a March 5, 1985, statement by Ambassador Robert B. Oakley, director of the State Department's Office for Counter-Terrorism and Emergency Planning, there are two main categories of Middle East terrorists: "Fanatical Palestinians who have split off from the mainline PLO (Palestine Liberation Organization) led by Arafat and often have the direct support of Libya, Syria and/or Iran; and Shia zealots from various Arab countries, especially Lebanon, who are inspired and trained, often armed and financed and, to varying degrees, guided by Iran." See U.S., House, Foreign Affairs Committee, *Combatting International Terrorism,* 99th Cong., 2nd sess., statement before the Subcommittees on Arms Control, International Security and Science, and International Operations, Current Policy No. 667, p. 2. See also Ambassador Oakley's address before the Issues Management Association, Chicago, Illinois, Spetember 13, 1985, U.S., Department of State, *Terrorism: Overview and Developments,* Current Policy No. 744, 5 pp.; U.S., Department of State, *International Terrorism,* Selected Documents No. 24, President Reagan's address to the nation, April 14, 1986 (this was the address announcing U.S. air strikes against Libya); U.S., Department of State, *Counterterrorism Policy,* statement by John Whitehead, deputy secretary

of state before the House Committee on Foreign Affairs, April 22, 1986, Current Policy No. 823, 3 pp.; William V. O'Brien, "Counterterrorism: Lessons from Israel," *Strategic Review* 13, no. 4 (Fall 1985): 32–44; and *Outthinking the Terrorist: An International Challenge,* Proceedings of the 10th Annual Symposium on the Role of Behavioral Science in Physical Security, Springfield, Virginia, April 23 and 24, 1985 (Washington, D.C.: Defense Nuclear Agency), 104 pp.

2. Historically, many violent acts of terrorist groups *have* alienated popular support and *have* been counterproductive to political objectives. It is worth pointing out, however, that the practice of terror and cruelty can occasionally elicit support and admiration as well as revulsion. In writing about the history of bandits, for example, Eric Hobsbawm has indicated that bandits have often become heroes not in spite of their terrible cruelty (cruelty, incidentally, beside which some examples of modern terrorism pale into insignificance), but because of it. The hero image stems not from their presumed ability to right wrongs, but to *avenge.* In describing the Colombian *violencia* during the peasant revolution of the years after 1948, Hobsbawm points out that bandits who chopped prisoners into tiny fragments before whole villages and ripped fetuses from pregnant women became instant heroes to the local population. See Eric Hobsbawm, *Bandits* (New York: Dell, 1969).

What this suggests, from the point of view of effective counter–nuclear terrorism, is that the ability to convince terrorist groups that higher-order acts of violence are apt to be self-defeating may be impossible in certain contexts. In such cases, in which resort to nuclear terrorism may actually generate admiration and support, efforts to prevent this terrorism must center on other bases of deterrence.

3. It is ironic that the mainspring of global security has always been the threat to punish rather than the promise to reward. After all, beginning with studies of child rearing, the literature on behavior modification regularly underscores the idea that positive sanctions are more effective than negative ones, that we can influence more flies with honey than with vinegar. In reference to reducing the probability of nuclear terrorism, we must begin to look at some carrots as well as the usual sticks.

4. Prior to the advent of concern for higher-order acts of terrorism, the idea that governments would engage in substantive bargaining with terrorists that might lead to major concessions was widely criticized. Today, however, we must face up to the fact that the execution of certain terrorist threats could have genuinely system-destructive effects. Recognizing this, the hard-line unwillingness to bargain and concede can no longer be regarded as a fixed and irrevocable position of responsible governments.

5. Some of the problems associated with such a strategy in a world system that is founded upon the principles of realpolitik concern the appearance of "bribes." Even if a strategy of positive sanctions is worked out that looks exceptionally promising, the public reaction to it may be exceedingly unfavorable. Matters of honor and courage, therefore, may mitigate against the operation of positive sanctions in counter-nuclear-terrorist strategies.

Another problem associated with the operation of positive sanctions in such strategies centers on the possibility that some terrorists who display a self-sacrificing value system thrive on violent action for its own sake. They are unconcerned with the political object or with matters of personal gain. Here, we are clearly up against a brick wall, the reductio ad absurdum of deterrence logic, because the only incentives that might be extended to deter acts of violence are the opportunities to commit such acts.

Then there is the "blackmail" problem. The habitual use of rewards to discourage terrorist violence is apt to encourage terrorists to extort an ever-expanding package of "gifts" in exchange for "good behavior." Here, we must confront the prospect of terrorism as a protection racket on a global scale.

6. A variation of this type of terrorist group is one in which the overarching motives are genuinely political, but in which ordinary criminality is engaged in to secure needed capital. Here, the primary activity of the group often centers on "expropriation," the long-established euphemism for robberies designed to supply terrorists with funds. The history of this tactic dates back to the Russian expropriators of the 1860s and 1870s. Later, Lenin was careful about maintaining a firm line between expropriations and ordinary crime, but today's expropriators have expressed far less concern about making a distinction. From the standpoint of effective counterterrorism, such diminished sensitivity is clearly desirable, because it makes it much easier for the government to equate the terrorist robberies with orthodox criminality.

7. See, for example, Ted Robert Gurr, *Why Men Rebel* (Princeton, N.J.: Princeton University Press, 1970), especially pp. 241–242, 259, and 274; Arnold H. Buss, *The Psychology of Aggression* (New York: Wiley, 1961), p. 58; and Leonard Berkowitz, *Aggression: A Social Psychological Analysis* (New York: McGraw-Hill, 1962), p. 96.

8. In this connection, governments must avoid the impression that the prospective costs of nuclear violence are so great as to warrant any and all concessions. Rather, prior to the onset of an actual incident, governments should create a hierarchy of concessions, ranging from the most easily satisfied financial demands to the most sweeping transformations of government policy and personnel. With such a hierarchy in hand, responsible officials could at least enter into a protracted bargaining situation with prospective nuclear terrorists, pursuing a concessionary policy that is both incremental and consistent with predetermined calculations of tolerable losses. Moreover, such preincident planning might also allow the government to take the offensive position in the bargaining situation.

9. Terrorists have long understood that harsh and repressive countermeasures often work in their own interests. With such an understanding, they have even developed tactics designed to goad governments into overreaction. In Algeria, FLN (National Liberation Front) strategy was designed to provoke the kind of countermeasures that would make compromise impossible. From the standpoint of effective counter-nuclear-terrorism strategies, these points suggest that governments give careful scrutiny to the prospective costs of harsh physical countermeasures before implementing such measures. Contrary to the facile conventional wisdom on the subject, fighting fire with fire is not always effective. Sometimes, it is much better to rely on water.

10. See Hannah Arendt, *On Violence* (New York: Harcourt Brace and World, 1970), p. 56.

11. It should not be assumed, however, that strategies of counter–nuclear terrorism that severely infringe civil liberties would necessarily be effective. The adoption of severe measures to curtail terrorism could impair civil liberties without providing any counterterrorist benefits. Indeed, such measures might even incite the very terrorist excesses they are designed to prevent.

12. Under international law, the range of protection granted to participants in noninternational armed conflicts has been steadily enlarged. The core of international legal protection for participants in internal wars is Article 3, common to the four Geneva Conventions of August 12, 1949, and two protocols to the conventions.

Protocol 1 makes the law concerning international conflicts applicable to conflicts fought for self-determination against alien occupation and against colonialist and racist regimes. A product of the Diplomatic Conference on the Reaffirmation and Development of International Humanitarian Law Applicable in Armed Conflicts that ended on June 10, 1977, the protocol (which was justified by the decolonization provisions of the UN Charter and by resolutions of the General Assembly) brings irregular forces within the full scope of the law of armed conflict. Protocol 2, also additional to the Geneva Conventions, concerns protection of victims of noninternational armed conflicts. Hence, this protocol applies to all armed conflicts that are not covered by Protocol 1 and that take place within the territory of a state between its armed forces and dissident armed forces. These dissident armed forces, to be under the jurisdiction of Protocol 2 and therefore of international law, must be "under responsible command" and "must exercise such control over a part of its territory as to enable them to carry out sustained and concerted military operations and to implement this Protocol."

13. Although every act of terrorism is clearly "criminal" insofar as it violates certain laws in the codes of particular jurisdictions, lacks "just cause" and/or violates the humanitarian rules of war, in the decision-making taxonomy the term "criminal" is applied only when robbery is adopted to secure funds.

14. Where such action is taken and prisoners taken, their status would not necessarily be the privileged one of lawful combatants. Under the Geneva Conventions of 1949, which reaffirm earlier principles of the Hague Regulations of 1899 and 1907 (and which are themselves reaffirmed by the two protocols of 1977), four requirements must be met to qualify for treatment as a prisoner of war: (1) be commanded by a person responsible for his subordinates; (2) have a fixed distinctive sign recognizable at a distance; (3) carry arms openly; and (4) conduct operations in accordance with the laws and customs of war. If these requirements are not met, the terrorist prisoners would not be due the benefits of privileged treatment.

15. Significantly, however, the U.S. Act to Combat International Terrorism (1984) defines "act of terrorism" as activity that (1) involves a violent act or an act dangerous to human life that is a violation of the criminal laws of the United States or of any state, or that would be a criminal violation if committed

within the jurisdiction of the United States or any of its states, and (2) appears to be intended to intimidate or coerce a civilian population, influence the policy of a government by intimidation or coercion, or to affect the conduct of a government by assassination or kidnapping. It follows that certain activities that might qualify as lawful insurgencies under the settled jurisprudential standards of international law would be treated under this statute as terrorism.

16. In terms of international law, as we have already noted, support for such sanctions can be found as far back as the eighteenth century in Emmerich de Vattel's *The Law of Nations.*

17. One attempt is built into the Final Document of the Conference on Terrorism and Political Crimes, June 4–16, 1972, Syracuse, Italy. According to Article 6 of this document:

1. The proposal to create such a court reaffirms a lengthy history on the subject, support for which has been expressed by distinguished jurists since the end of World War I, and was manifested in the 1937 Convention on the Prevention and Punishment of Terrorism and the two draft conventions elaborated by United Nations Committees in 1951 and 1953.
2. It is recommended once again that such a court be established with jurisdiction over international crimes and in particular over acts falling within the definition of terrorism.
3. A draft statute for such a court should be elaborated at the earliest opportunity, taking into consideration several existing proposals and in particular the proposed 1953 United Nations draft. Such a statute should also include questions of enforcement and sanctions.
4. The court should exercise its jurisdiction over persons and corporate entities but not over states, since questions involving states are within the jurisdiction of the International Court of Justice.
5. The proposed International Criminal Court could be created by the United Nations or be an organ thereof, as in the case of the International Court of Justice, or be independently created and operated as an autonomous international body. The realization of such a proposal could be by virtue of:
   a. a single multilateral treaty-statute;
   b. multilateral treaties on this and other subjects;
   c. bilateral treaties;
   d. amending protocols to existing international conventions;
   e. unilateral declarations;
   f. enactment of national legislation; or,
   g. voluntary submission to the jurisdiction of such Court or any other special arrangement.

See M. Cherif Bassiouni, *International Terrorism and Political Crimes* (Springfield, Ill.: C. C. Thomas, 1975), pp. xviii–xix.

18. One recent attempt to deal with the political-exception problem is the Supplemental Extradition Treaty between the United States and Great Britain, which was ratified by the U.S. Senate in July 1986. Prior to passage of this treaty, U.S. courts had refused to extradite alleged Irish Republican Army gunmen on the ground that an uprising exists in Northern Ireland that makes crimes committed in furtherance of the revolt "political." For an excellent

assessment of these issues, see Abraham D. Sofaer, "Terrorism and the Law," *Foreign Affairs* 64, no. 5 (Summer 1986): 901–922. See also Abraham D. Sofaer, "The Political Offense Exception and Terrorism," U.S. Department of State, Current Policy No. 762, a statement by the Legal Adviser, to the Department of State before the Senate Foreign Relations Committee, August 1, 1985, 5 pp. For an important earlier assessment of this problem and associated issues concerning law and counterterrorism, see John F. Murphy, *Legal Aspects of International Terrorism: Summary Report of an International Conference,* American Society of International Law, December 13–15, 1978, U.S. Department of State (St. Paul, Minn.: West Publishing Company, 1980).

19. This distinction lies at the heart of U.S.-Soviet differences on terrorism. From the Soviet perspective, the United States uses the term "terrorism" to discredit what they regard as essential and legitimate movements for self-determination. In the words of a recent Soviet publication by I. Blischenko and N. Zhdanov, *Terrorism and International Law* (Moscow: Progress Publishers, 1984), p. 10: "Representatives of imperialist States attempt to exploit the discussion of 'international terrorism' in the UN in order to extend this concept to the national liberation struggle and to various forms of the class struggle of the working people for their rights." In their view, of course, the insurgent use of force against regimes the United States freely calls "authoritarian" (for example, El Salvador, Chile, South Africa) does not display "terrorism" (the U.S. position) but "national liberation." Moreover, U.S. assistance to insurgent forces seeking to topple pro-Soviet regimes (for example, Nicaragua, Angola) displays not "freedom fighting" (the U.S. position) but "state-supported terrorism."

From the U.S. perspective, the Soviet Union uses the term "terrorist" to discredit what the United States regards as authentic movements for freedom and democracy. In the official U.S. view, the insurgent use of force against "totalitarian" regimes represents genuine support for movements of national liberation and self-determination. Moreover, Soviet assistance to insurgent forces seeking to topple pro-U.S. regimes seeks only to "spread chaos and subversion." Hence, such assistance is alleged to flow not from a Soviet commitment to national liberation or self-determination, but from an ingrained habit of nurturing terrorism.

20. See Elie Wiesel, *A Jew Today* (New York: Random House, 1978), p. 94.

21. Ibid., p. 95.

22. The spurious notion that every anti-Communist insurgency is an instance of freedom fighting did not originate with the Reagan administration. At the end of World War II, when the United States conducted its "operation Ratline," even Nazi war criminals were put to work in East Germany and in the Soviet Union as instruments of the free world. Although this disgraceful episode in U.S. history was intended to be kept secret (rather than displayed openly in the fashion of current support for contra and Unita terrorists), it reveals the humiliating and self-defeating measures we are willing to embrace as "geopolitical necessities." Can this country seriously contend with the threat of nuclear terrorism while it attempts to convince the world that its own support for Nazis and thugs is "in defense of freedom"? Significantly, current support for the

contras and Unita comes, in part, from neo-Nazi groups throughout the world and from the remnants of Nazi-collaborator extermination units in Europe.

23. Ironically, Secretary of State Schultz has often stated his commitment to the laws of war of international law and to the understanding that these humanitarian rules of armed conflict apply as well to insurgent forces. According to Schultz: "The grievances that terrorists supposedly seek to redress through acts of violence may or may not be legitimate. The terrorist acts themselves, however, can never be legitimate. And legitimate causes can never justify or excuse terrorism. Terrorist means discredit their ends." See U.S., Department of State, Bureau of Public Affairs, "Terrorism and the Modern World," Current policy No. 629, October 25, 1984, p. 3.

24. In addition to the *territorial principle* and the *nationality principle,* there are three other traditionally recognized bases of jurisdiction under international law: the *protective principle,* determining jurisdiction by reference to the national interest injured by the offense; the *universality principle,* determining jurisdiction by reference to the custody of the person committing the offense; and the *passive personality principle,* determining jurisdiction by reference to the nationality of the person injured by the offense.

25. The assumption that every Marxist state must be considered an enemy of this country—an assumption that underlies the Reagan Doctrine—is unsupported by historical evidence. We need only consider the cases of China, Yugoslavia, and Romania to understand that Communist states evolve and that they need not remain unalterably opposed to the United States. Indeed, the evidence should also be appraised from the standpoint of the Soviet Union, an appraisal that would have promising implications for increasing U.S.-Soviet cooperation.

26. Although the conditions of cold war compel the Soviets to support various insurgencies (both lawful and lawless), the philosophic foundations of the USSR actually oppose terrorism. In a speech at the Congress of the Social-Democratic Party of Switzerland on November 4, 1916, Lenin stated: "We stand by our old conviction, confirmed by experience over decades, that individual terrorist acts are *inexpedient* methods of political struggle. . . . Only the mass movement can be considered genuine political struggle." Recent Soviet writers have reaffirmed this view. For example, according to Blischchenko and Zhdanov, the individual acts of terror we witness today are "peculiar to the petty-bourgeois groups and those sections of intellectuals who do not have the support of a particular class to rely on" (*Terrorism and International Law,* p. 31). We may also extrapolate from the authors' approving references to Lenin's views on terrorism that the Soviet Union remains opposed, at least for tactical reasons, to the very sorts of terror to which the United States routinely ascribes Soviet support.

Doctrinally, the Soviets today have no faith in terrorist violence. From their perspective, such violence reveals a spontaneous character (a very negative feature) and a "divorce from the masses." Indeed, terrorism is foredoomed because it is "subjective," because it represents what Lenin identified as the "result of a lack of faith in insurrection" and "the absence of conditions" for insurrection. Or as Georgi Plekhanov has written: "So-called terrorism is not a proletarian method of struggle. . . . The true terrorist is an individualist by nature (very negative feature) or by 'circumstances beyond his control.'" See "A.I. Herzen and Serfdom," Selected Philosophical Works, 5 vols. vol. 5 (Moscow: Progress Publishers, 1981), p. 467.

Today the Soviet Union officially regards terrorism of the extreme Left as an expression of petty-bourgeois ideology and "adventurism." Not surprisingly, therefore, they have chosen to condemn as terrorists the very groups the United States repeatedly claims act as their surrogates. Recent Soviet publications, for example, have included as terrorists the Japanese Red Army, the Italian Red Brigades, Direct Action in France, and the Red Army Faction in Germany. In their view, such forms of terror are counterproductive because they are advanced as an independent type of action divorced from the class political struggle. Accepting the Marxist idea that only mass movement can be considered genuine political struggle, they assert that terrorism does nothing but serve the interests of "reaction."

Chapter 6

1. The connection seems to have been understood in a special light by Herbert Marcuse. Although not speaking about international politics directly, Marcuse recognized the paradoxical and self-defeating efforts of "society" to impose principles of nonviolence on the opposition while systematically enlarging its arena of "legitimate" violence. Understood in terms of the problem of nuclear terrorism, the philosopher's wisdom suggests a clear nexus between the state's characteristic mode of security seeking and the penchant for terrorist violence. See Herbert Marcuse, *Counterrevolution and Revolt* (Boston: Beacon Press, 1972), p. 52.

2. See William Irwin Thompson, *Passages About Earth: An Exploration of the New Planetary Culture* (New York: Harper and Row, 1974), pp. 131–132.

3. See Jonas Salk, *The Survival of the Wisest* (New York: Harper and Row, 1973), p. 82.

4. Kierkegaard's and Nietzsche's views on self-affirmation have points in common with Paul Tillich and the existential psychotherapist Rollo May. Tillich speaks of this quality as the "courage to be." Without this courage, a person loses "being." Commenting upon the essential characteristics that constitute a person, May refers to the importance of "preserving one's centeredness." In both sets of views, the emphasis is on creating and preserving identity, but not at the expense of fruitful participation with other beings. The goal is always to actualize human potentialities in harmony with others. See, for example, Paul Tillich, *The Courage to Be* (New Haven: Yale University Press, 1952) and Rollo May, "Existential Bases of Psychotherapy," in Rollo May, ed., *Existential Psychology* (New York: Random House, 1961).

5. From the standpoint of post–World War II history, there has been a steady shift from an initial era of bipolarity to one of multipolarity. The actual time of the transfer, however, is a matter of continuing disagreement among statesmen and scholars.

6. Although the balance of power appears to have offered two relatively peaceful periods in history—the periods beginning with the Peace of Westphalia and the Congress of Vienna—the hundred-year interval between the Napoleonic wars and World War I was actually a period of frequent wars in Europe. The fact that the balance of power has been disastrously ineffective in producing peace during our own century hardly warrants mention.

7. Contrariwise, it has been argued persuasively that equilibrium heightens the danger of war by giving all parties the impression of possible victory, whereas disequilibrium deters the weaker sides while the stronger ones lack incentive.

8. This is because there is nothing about the new balance system that is able to ensure the credibility of particular deterrence postures. In its mistaken orientation to notions of selective equilibrium and the prevention of hegemony, multipolarism thus ignores the truly essential basis of peaceful international relations in a world system that lacks government. It goes almost without saying that multipolarism also ignores a number of other grievously dangerous risks to security, some of which are unrelated to the "deadly logic" of deterrence. These risks are in the form of accidental nuclear war, nuclear war that is precipitated by unauthorized individuals, and nuclear war that results from incorrect calculations concerning reciprocity.

9. See Wolfram E. Hanrieder, "The International System: Bipolar or Multibloc," *Journal of Conflict Resolution* 9 (September 1965): 299–308.

10. Historically, of course, a balance of power system was ushered in with the Peace of Westphalia in 1648 and has been with us ever since. The basic dynamics of this system were reaffirmed at the Peace of Utrecht in 1713; the Congress of Vienna in 1815; and the settlements following the two world wars. Strictly speaking, neither the League of Nations nor the United Nations can qualify as a system of collective security. Rather, both are examples of international organization functioning within a balance of power world. As for world government, even the case of Imperial Rome does not, strictly speaking, fulfill the appropriate criteria, because the extent of its jurisdiction was coextensive with only a portion of the entire world.

11. Among the most widely known exponents of this idea in the history of Western political thought are the following: Dante, *De Monarchia;* Georg Podebrad's planned federation of Christian princes; Pope Leo's proposal; Francois de la Noue, *Discours politiques et militaries;* Emeric Crucé, *Nouveau Cyneé;* Sully, *Le Grand Dessein;* William Penn, *An Essay Towards the Present and Future Peace of Europe by the Establishment of an European Diet, Parliament,* or *Estates;* John Bellers, *Some Reasons for a European State Proposed to the Powers of Europe;* C. I. Castel de Saint-Pierre, *Projet de paix perpetuelle;* Jean Jacques Rousseau, *A Lasting Place Through the Federation of Europe;* Jeremy Bentham, *Plan for an Universal and Perpetual Peace;* Immanuel Kant, *Zum ewigen Frieden.*

A vast literature advancing the case for world centralization has its origins in our century. Among the most notable are the following: Raymond L. Bridgman, *World Organization* (1905); H. G. Wells, *The Common Sense of World Peace* (1929); Clarence K. Streit, *For Union Now* (1939); W. B. Curry, *The Case for a Federal Union* (1939); David Hoadley Munroe, *Hang Together: The Union Now*

Primer (1940); Grenville Clark, *A Memorandum With Regard to a New Effort to Organize Peace* (1939); Duncan and Elizabeth Wilson, *Federation and World Order* (1939); Oscar Newfang, *World Government* (1942); Emery Reves, *Anatomy of Peace* (1945); Norman Cousins, *Modern Man is Obsolete* (1945); Cord Meyer, *Peace or Anarchy* (1947); Crane Brinton, *From Many One* (1948); Vernon Nash, *The World Must Be Governed* (1949); Grenville Clark and Louis B. Sohn, *World Peace Through World Law* (1966); Richard A. Falk, *A Study of Future Worlds* (1975); and Saul H. Mendlovitz, *On the Creation of a Just World Order* (1975).

12. The distinguished psychiatrist, Jerome D. Frank, has pointed out, "At least seventy-five chiefs of state in the last four centuries led their countries while suffering from several mental disturbances." See Frank, *Sanity and Survival, Psychological Aspects of War and Peace* (New York: Random House, 1967), p. 59.

13. May 22, 1977.

Index

ABM. *See* Antiballistic missile
Achille Lauro (Italian ship), 90, 92, 93
Act for the Prevention and Punishment of the Crime of Hostage-Taking (1984), 88
Act to Combat International Terrorism (1984), 88, 140–141(n15)
Ad Hoc Committee on International Terrorism (1973) (UN), 4, 91
Afghanistan, 95
Aggression, Definition of (1974) (UN), 4, 71, 91
Agriculture, 47
Aircraft Sabotage Act (1984), 88
Albright, David, 19
Alexander (king of Yugoslavia), 31
ALF. *See* Arab Liberation Front
Algeria, 90
Algiers (Algeria), 90
"America and the Struggle for Freedom" (Shultz), 10
American Convention on Human Rights, 88
Anarchy, 119
Angola, 31, 75, 76
Angst, 55, 103
Antarctic Treaty (1961), 65
Antiballistic missile (ABM), 60
Antichrist (Nietzsche), 35
Anti-Sovietism, 11, 12, 13, 14, 62, 72, 73–74, 76, 93, 94, 95, 101–102, 104, 105, 142–143(n22)
Apartheid, 11, 12, 76, 126(n14)
Apocalyptic possibilities, 36
Aquatic life, 46, 47

Arab Liberation Front (ALF), 89
Arab states, 30, 65
Arafat, Yasir, 7, 89
Arendt, Hannah, 7, 26, 73, 81
Argentina, 68
Aristotle, 5, 24, 25, 48
Arms control, 60, 64, 94. *See also* Nonproliferation
Arms race, 3, 59, 98, 123
Atomic Energy Act (1954), 59
Auschwitz, 31
Aut dedere aut punire. See Extradite or prosecute principle
Authoritarian regimes, 11, 74, 75, 82, 95

Baader-Meinhof group, 29
Bakhunin, Mikhail, 7, 26
Balance of payments, 67
Balance of power, 107, 108, 118–119, 145(nn 6, 10)
Ballistic missiles, 37, 133–134(n4)
defense (BMD), 60, 133–134(n4)
"Banality of evil," 26
Bargaining, 79, 138(n4)
Behavioral strategy
appraisals, 78, 80, 81, 83–87
and civil liberties, 81–83
concessions, 79, 80, 85(table), 86
international, 87–95, 97
positive sanctions, 79, 80–81, 83, 84, 85(table), 86, 138–139(n5)
retaliation, 79–80, 85(table), 86, 87
and risk calculations, 77–78, 80, 81, 82
Bigney, Russell E., 31